Alfred Morris

Passing Thoughts in Verse

Alfred Morris

Passing Thoughts in Verse

ISBN/EAN: 9783337811303

Printed in Europe, USA, Canada, Australia, Japan

Cover: Foto ©Thomas Meinert / pixelio.de

More available books at **www.hansebooks.com**

PASSING THOUGHTS

PASSING THOUGHTS

In Verse

BY

ALFRED MORRIS

London

T. FISHER UNWIN

1896

LOAN STACK

To the

OLD BOYS OF S. MARK'S SCHOOL, HOLLOWAY,

THIS LITTLE WORK IS AFFECTIONATELY

INSCRIBED.

109

CONTENTS.

8		*CONTENTS.*

IN MEMORIAM, E. A. G. 88
REMEMBRANCES 90
EMIGRANTS 92
THE WIND 99
A LANDSCAPE 101
THE BASS-VIOL 103
IN MEMORIAM, REV. C. L. VAUGHAN . . 107
AURORA BOREALIS 109
SLEEP 111
ALLELUIA ! 114
WHAT IS SORROW ? 116
EVENTIDE 118
THE EVERLASTING HILLS 119
THE LITTLE GRAVE 121
IN MEMORIAM, A. M. 123
THE SEAMLESS ROBE 125
"AND THERE WAS NO MORE SEA" . . 126
A LAMENT. 128
CHRISTMAS 130
A CHRISTMAS WISH 132
EASTER 134
ASCENSION DAY 136
CHILDREN'S FESTAL HYMN 138
"GRANT US THY PEACE" 140
HYMN AT THE LAYING OF THE FOUNDATION
	STONE OF A MISSION HALL . . . 142
HYMN AT THE DEDICATION OF A MISSION HALL 144
LITANY FOR S. ALBAN'S DAY 146
LITANY FOR A BOYS' GUILD 148

TO THE READER.

"A SMALL craft," you will say, "and certain of shipwreck by the breath of criticism." It may be so, and yet, with many misgivings, it is launched with the humble hope that in its cargo may be found something to revivify the Past with pleasant memories, to interest and perhaps instruct in the Present, and to raise happy anticipations for the Future.

A. M.

EASTERTIDE, 1896.

PASSING THOUGHTS.

STRANGE passing thoughts! that fluttering fall
    apace,
  Like flakes of winter snow,
To hide the winding path we trace
  Beneath a garb of woe!

That rest on graves where love long buried lies,
  Recalling faces dear,
As minor chords breathe tender sighs
  Upon the listful ear.

Those passing thoughts! that flit like autumn leaves,
  And tell of fleeting years,
Of devious ways the heart retrieves
  In penitential tears.

Those passing thoughts! that bring the chime of
    bells
  Back from the days of yore;
Our childhood in the music dwells
  That echoes evermore.

Our passing thoughts would scan the future way,
   And, while the seed is sown,
Anticipate the final day
   When reapers claim their own ;

When God, Eternal, yet Who grows not old,
   Gives ever youthful life,
And crowns in spring's eternal fold
   Each victor in the strife.

Perchance the passing thoughts may then retrace
   Life's journey of unrest,
Revealing mercy, goodness, grace,
   All working for the best.

LAURA.

THE Manor House a pile of grandeur stood
'Mid "tall ancestral trees." The swallows built
Year after year beneath its massive eaves,
And man succeeded man in ownership,
While ivy leaves grew high and higher still,
Till all the walls were cloth'd in shining green.
A good old home in very truth it was,—
So old, indeed, that solemnising thoughts
Perforce would rise within the stranger's mind,
As first he stood within its ancient hall,—
E'en as cathedral's lofty arch and aisle
The spirit of frivolity dispel.
And yet fair childhood's laughter wak'd around
The echoes sleeping in those stern old walls,
And sent sweet music ringing through the halls
And rolling down the lengthen'd corridors.
The old, old hearth that told of those long since
Departed, who had sought its welcome blaze,
The faded pictures on the gloomy walls,
The tatter'd banners hanging far aloft,
The rusty armour plac'd in every niche,—
All seem'd to frown upon the joyous notes,
And make that ringing laugh as out of place
As joy at grief, or mirth around the dead.

But in the woods fair Laura's laugh attuned
With songs of birds—in harmony with all.
When childhood's days had worn themselves away,
Her leisure time was spent amid the flowers
That deck'd her garden ground. She oft would
    seek
The rustic seat beneath the spreading elm,
And with a favourite book would while away
The hours in sweet forgetfulness of self.
Methinks the merry songsters of the grove
Their joyous chorus rais'd for her dear sake,
And flowers, because she lov'd them all so well,
Unfurl'd their beauties to the summer sun.
The simple cottagers around all knew
And prais'd the generous spirit that was hers.
Of her old dames would talk away an hour,
Commenting in no measur'd terms of love
On all her works of love,—how, angel-like,
In visits to the sick, her gentle hand
Had smooth'd the pillow, where the fever'd brain
In vain sought healing rest,—how she had cheer'd
The sad with loving, gladsome words,—how help'd
The fallen child and kiss'd the pain away.
Of those they'd tell who had assistance got
From her large bounty,—those whom her kind
    heart
From slandrous wrongs had shelter'd,—lingering
    still
On ev'ry detail of the visits paid.
And thus the world, half envious of her lot,
Declar'd hers was a life without a cloud.

The world was wrong. The heart alone can know
The bitterness within.
                    The doting love
Of gentle mother, like the springtide sun
On primrose banks, brought out a sweet response
Of loving deeds in Laura's tender heart.
Love gender'd love, and love grew more and more
Till childhood's years were waning. Then a shroud
Of lingering sorrow cast deep shadows o'er
Long days to come—long days when Laura miss'd
Her mother's fond caress, and mother's love
Had left in aching heart a dreary void
That nought could fill, save envy of the child
Who took its little cares and sorrows light
To draw sweet solace from its mother's heart.

Her father, seldom home, seem'd scarce to know
His daughter lived. Upon his soul had hung
A cloud of disappointment since her birth.
He crav'd a son to bear his name and take
In next succession all his large estate.
And now 'twas rumour'd that he sought again,
In second wedded life, to find fulfill'd
The yearning hope that died at Laura's birth.

And thus, with heart that longed for kindred heart,
With love that only lived upon the past,
And in the present found no resting-place,
What wonder if in Laura's soul should spring

A fount of love for Ellington's young squire—
For him whose manly tenderness had soothed,
Whose looks of love drew love up by the roots,
Whose words breath'd peace upon the troubled
    heart,
Who'd promis'd love till death.

                      And they were wed.
The village bells ne'er rang in noisier glee,
And village dames ne'er richer blessings call'd
On happy bride, and never children's hands
More lovingly the scattering flow'rets threw
Than those at Laura's wedding. Here was made
No gaudy show, but in the Church's rite
The villagers were one in earnest prayer,
And pleaded in the wedding Eucharist
For all best blessings on the wedded pair.
And loving prayers were answer'd in the love
That lighted up the home of Ellington,—
Were answer'd too when death had snapp'd the
    bond,
For heaven-born love in heaven alone can thrive,
And all good prayers find fullest answer there.

Not many moons had shone upon the scene,
And he was called away in trustful hope,
Commending her to God's abiding love.
But oh ! the strain on Laura's breaking heart,
The anguish pains that rack'd its very depths,
The aching grief in midnight's solemn hour,
The wearying watches many a sad night through,

The never-ceasing flood of bitter tears !
The heart again alone its bitterness
Could know.
         Time ton'd the sorrow down, and hope
Wove loving garlands round the heavy cross.
The child—the lov'd unconscious innocent—
Expelled the darkness from his mother's heart.
For him she lived, in him was her delight,
And as she kiss'd her darling little one
Full oft, from deepest depths of mother's love,
Would summon all the most endearing names
To heap in them that changeless love on him.
What music was there in his lisping voice,
What sunshine in his happy face of smiles,
What pleasure by maternal duties given !

But all too soon the brightness died away,
And, like a springtide frost on tender bud,
Dread sickness fell ! The lisping voice was
    hush'd,
No sunny smile play'd on the little face !
Ah ! who can tell of Laura's anxious care
And vigils sad beside her little one !
A mother's never-ceasing heaven-like love
For each dear child is unapproachable,
Yet even this is ten times multiplied
On one that sickness robbeth of its play.
Her ev'ry care is then to please and make
Affliction light. How many times will her
Caress smooth ev'ry pain away, and, when
In silent night the world is hush'd, how she

Will rouse at ev'ry stir and minister
To ev'ry want, nor dream of selfish rest
And ease, so long as they do not attend
On her sick child. And ten times this the love's
Increased if that frail one's the only child—
The only thing on this cold earth in which
That parent's love expecteth a return.—
And even ten times this was Laura's love
For her sick child !

              And day by day she watch'd,
And night by night she waited for the dawn,
As dim and dimmer still hope's star burn'd on,
While sad and slow the old clock's ticks gave
    pulse
To sorrow, till in early morning hour
The parting strife drew near, and with a sigh—
A gentle sigh—the unpolluted soul
Of Laura's child pass'd from the earth away,
To join the band of Holy Innocents,—
Fair flow'rets sparkling with Baptismal dew—
And swell the loud Hosannahs rais'd to Him
Who changeth troubled rest on mother's breast
For His dear love and angel's sheltering wing.

But in that chamber all was still, save when
The deep convulsive sob from Laura's heart
Arose, as there in bitter grief she knelt
And vainly strove in that lov'd form to kiss
The parted spirit back again. Then sleep,
A restless slumber, seal'd the weeping eyes—

In sorrow Laura slept.   But misty dreams
Brought back again the scenes of early days.
The Manor House and old acquaintances
Surroundings made, while once again the love
Of noble heart was told and told again,
Till Laura's heavy sigh effaced the scene.
And now, as if in contrast, in her dream
Her days on earth have well-nigh worn away,
And she is old, with hair of silver white
And time's deep furrows trac'd upon her face ;
The step is feeble and the eyes are dim,
Yet one in love the closer to her clings,
Delights to call her " mother," and to see
Her ev'ry wish fulfill'd.   He is her son—
The babe, the little babe, that sleeping lies
In death's embrace.   She sees him grown a man,
Robust and tall, with sunny countenance
That beams in smiles on her. His strong, firm arm
Supports her in the rambles she can take,
And in the tiny vine-spread summer-house,
Her wearied limbs at rest, his kindly words
Are music to her heart, and bless the life
Of second infancy.   And here again
A sigh of deepest agony burst forth,
And Laura woke.   At rest before her was
The sleeping form of that dear little one
Who, grown a man, had tended in her dream.
A smile was fixed upon its little face,
In welcome perhaps to some bright angel form
That came to bear the little soul away.
The sight drove Laura back again to tears,

Till once again she wept herself to sleep.
And then a smile of radiant sweetness play'd,
Like rainbow on the cloud, upon her face,
For now she saw her infant once again,
Not dead and ready for the chilling grave,
But bright and happy with the beautiful,
Where robes of light, bright golden crowns, and
  harps
Of sweetest melody rejoice the throng,
That dwells on that e'er-flowering, deathless shore.
His loving smile bade her approach his bliss,
But surging waters darkly roll'd between,
And murky darkness veil'd the vision's light !
The dreamer wept, and, weeping, woke again.

The weary days, the sleepless nights were years
To Laura. Grass had cloth'd the tiny mound.
And now the chilling wintry winds howl'd through
The leafless woods, while gathering clouds hid
  stars
And heaven's pale moon. A figure glided o'er
The dismal fields of Ellington, of cold
And storm regardless—passing on with song
That echo'd in the wakeful rustic's ear
In silent hours when earth was wrapped in sleep !
Frail Laura heeded not the gathering storm !
'Though closely watch'd, yet had she now con-
  triv'd
Escape from careful keeper's vigilance !
In sadden'd hearts her cry will never cease—
The bitter cry of piteous pleading vain,

That she might go to join her little one.
In vain she told how infant voice allur'd,
How infant hand was beckoning her to rest,
And begged with burning tears that she might go
And wander free to once again embrace
Her dear one in the love of mother's heart !

The morn began a cold, cold day, when snow—
The midnight snow—a chilling robe, had cloth'd
The landscape o'er. The keepers found too late
The maniac inmate of the Hall had gone—
Had wander'd from the house, they knew not
    where !
They trac'd the footsteps in the snow, they trac'd
Them on through woods, o'er frozen stream, the
    road,
The by-path to the old churchyard, and there,
Upon a tiny mound, dead Laura slept
In that last sleep which has no waking hour
Until the ringing trump of God shall rouse
All from the dead to sleep again no more.

MOTHER CHURCH.

Commission'd by its Lord, forth went the band
To rear the Holy Church in ev'ry land,
To sow the precious seed in martyrs' tears,
That sheaves of bliss might crown the after years,
And in this wilderness a table spread
To feed the fainting with the Living Bread !

From thence our Mother Church, with ceaseless
    care,
For England's sons has scattered everywhere
The flowers of grace, to cheer through paths of
    life
The faithful hearts undaunted in the strife—
Brave hearts that follow on in narrow way
Till dawns the fulness of the perfect day !

She gives her benison on Eden's rose—
The love of wedded pain—and Heaven's grace
    flows
That they, in mystic rite made man and wife,
A mutual help may be in chequer'd life—
Their love an image of the union blest
'Twixt Christ and those who in His love find rest.

22

And when the firstborn heralds grateful joy,
When hope's fair flow'rets crown the baby boy,
His mother for her " Churching" meekly kneels,
As from her full glad heart uprising steals,
In words subdued, amid the chancel's calm,
The incense fragrance of her thankful psalm.

Her boy she bringeth to the sacred flood
That speaks of cleansing and the Precious Blood,
Where grace from birth-sin makes the sin-stain'd
    whole,
And God in mercy claims the new-born soul.
The Holy Sign of Faith and service here,
Of mighty aid when threefold foes are near,
Is made upon the infant's brow, that he
Christ's faithful soldier evermore may be ;
And kneeling worshippers devoutly pray
The little one, kept safe in narrow way,
May, when the storms of life are past,
In God's eternal kingdom rest at last.

Full soon the boy's first lisping prayers ascend,
And with his growing life instructions blend.
The Catechism and the holy lore
The Church's daily lessons ever pour
Make Faith and Duty for the pathway clear,
And hymns of faith the pilgrim footsteps cheer.
Through Feast and Fast the Gospel story's told,
Repeated ever, ever new, though old,
And balmy as the breath of summer flowers
Whose fragrance lingers round the passing hours.

On rapid wing comes round the solemn hour
In which the sevenfold gift of Spirit's dower
Descends in Confirmation grace. By bishop's hand
A place he takes in royal priesthood band.

Next comes the happiest, sweetest time of bliss,
When eastern tints the dewy hill-tops kiss,
And eastern rays through eastern window-pane
On tesselated pavement paint again
The rainbow colours—such as John Divine
Saw compassing the heavenly Altar Shrine.
Before earth's altar kneels the trembling boy
With downcast eyes, while floods of holy joy
Suffuse his raptured soul from highest heaven,
As in dear Sacrament his Lord is given.
Oh! joy, all joys beyond, in First Communion blest
In Jesus' love to find the heart's true rest,
While grateful love adoring overflows,
And all the sweetness of His Presence knows.

Year after year in rapid flight succeeds ;
The means of grace supply the longing needs
Of him in manhood's strength. Then fades the
        day,
The evening shadows o'er the landscape stray,
And tottering steps can reach God's house no
        more.
Then Mother Church goes forth with comfort's
        store
In "Visitation of the Sick."   Her vested priest
By bedside makes her Eucharistic Feast,

Where soul and body from life-giving Food
All strength receive when death's dark shadows
  brood,
And when frail body yields its last long sigh,
Commends the passing soul to God on high.

E'en then her work of love is not complete !
Her white-rob'd throng goes forth the dead to
  meet ;
She chants aloud her resurrection lay
Of endless rest and glory's deathless day.
With words of life and love around the bier
She brings to stricken hearts hope's quickening
  cheer ;
Her holy dead then from her portal takes,
In holy ground his resting-place she makes,
Imploring her dear Lord with earnest cry
To bring His everlasting kingdom nigh.

Thus when the pilgrim's race by grace is run,
And anxious toiling on life's way is done,
Her sleepy child, by weariness oppress'd,
With sweetest lullaby she soothes to rest.
From font to grave the pilgrim way she tends,
Adds joy to joy, in sorrow comfort lends,
To troubled hearts a kindly foretaste brings
Of her true home where song of angels rings,
Shows forth the day when warriors' strife is o'er,
And conquerors reign in triumph evermore.

THE SONG OF THE OWL.

I SIT alone in the ivied tower,
  In the gloomiest shade it knows,
And much do I love in that darksome bower
  My place of dull repose.

I sit alone all the livelong day,
  And mope as hours roll by,
Till western tints have died away,
  Then off in the dark I fly.

I love the gloom of the darkest night,
  When earth is wrapp'd in sleep,
And dark arcades are my delight,
  Where moonbeams never peep.

In solitude the bright day long
  I roost where church bells ring,
While busy birds their careless song
  O'er hill and valley fling.

While the ploughman's plough turns up the sod,
  And shepherds tend their sheep,
While th' weary travellers onward plod
  In cool retreat I sleep.

But night, dark night, is a joy to me,
  No tim'rous fears have I,
As forth for sport and revelry
  On noiseless wing I fly.

Though winds may howl around my bower
  Above the churchyard trees,
Secure I sleep in the crumbling tower
  That moans with ev'ry breeze.

When the sad cold moon in sadness beams
  On fallow land and lea,
A rushing flight o'er woods and streams
  Is joy indeed for me.

For years and years have I liv'd alone,
  And many a strange sight seen,
Few know as I each crumbling stone,
  Or go where I have been.

     To-whit ! To-whoo !
     The dark woods through,
     'Tis merry sport to me !
     The darkest night
     And moon's sad light
     Alike shall share my glee !

'Twas when the wind blew loud and strong,
With dismal howls the woods among,
I, on my rapid, noiseless flight,
Forth darted in the gloom of night.

The rays of not a single star
Could pierce the darkness spread afar ;
Yet from the cot in Willow Lane
One flickering light from window pane
Told where th' old shepherd, wan and pale,
Was finishing life's weary tale,
And panting breath died on the breeze
That sigh'd and whistled through the trees.
The candle show'd a winding-sheet,
In measur'd ticks the death-watch beat,
And I, to give my omen too,
Against the lattic'd window flew
With shriek that floated on the gale
Adown the haunted Willow Vale.
  For abroad I fly,
  And for naught care I.
  The howling gale,
  The piteous wail,
  And midnight drear
  Give never a fear
As, when on my errands of mystery,
My shrieks and the wind make minstrelsy !

From lofty perch in ivied tree,
In night as black as night can be,
I've watched go forth a funeral train—
Not to the churchyard's hallow'd fane !
I saw men dig in dead of night,
Beneath the lantern's feeble light,
Unhallow'd grave in broad highway,
And there a corpse unhallow'd lay !

'Twas strange to me
That such should be,
But nought I fear
That's dread and drear ;
Whatever horrors night may know,
No sign of terror will I show !

The world was still, and summer flowers
Were hung with dew of midnight hours ;
Beneath my home each grassy blade
And leaflet in the willow glade
Stirr'd not to mark the zephyr's flight,
So calm, so tranquil was the night.
Short time before the sexton old
Had dug a grave ; the bell had toll'd,
The solemn funeral rites were done,
And fitful rays of setting sun
Fell chequer'd 'neath the willow's wave
Upon another new-made grave.
I watch'd it now, as cautious men
In dead of night brought forth again,
Scarce visible in midnight gloom,
The tenant of that darksome tomb !
They bore it hence, I know not where ;
I know not, and I do not care !
　　　To-whit !　To-whoo !
　　　The whole night through !
'Mong dismal tombs in churchyard drear
With ghosts and goblins I've no fear !

I've known the sexton old and grey,
  Who toils the graves among ;
I've seen him watch the night away ;
  I knew him young and strong !

And still his busy work ne'er stays,
  Grave after grave is made ;
Toilsome and many are his days,
  Yet well he plies his spade.

He digs for young, he digs for old,
  And digs without a care,
Nor thinks that he in churchyard mould
  Full soon a place shall share.

And when he trudges home at night,
  His tottering step I see,
And feel he only has the right
  To share the gloom with me !

The sexton, church, and haunted vale,
The winds that breathe a mournful wail,
The ivied tower and hollow tree
Content and pleasure yield for me !
    When the moonbeams fall
    'Cross the shadowy hall,
    And the chill winds blow,
    Then flying I go,
    With my whit-to-whoo,
    The long night through !

"UNTIL THE EVENING."

A CHARM is in the early hours
When morning wakes the sleeping flowers,
And, slowly rising o'er the hill,
The golden sun begins to fill
The world with life and busy sound,
And gladsome glory flings around.
There's joy when, in his noontide pride,
His splendour casts the mists aside,
Suffusing all with floods of gold,
And scattering brilliant gems untold
Upon old ocean's azure breast,
And on the snowy mountain's crest ;
When insects flit on gauzy wing,
While larks in highest heaven sing,
And fitful gleams, in fairy bands,
Are dancing through the forest lands.
But best of all the setting sun
That gilds the west when day is done,
That gives to weary toil a rest,
That breathes a calm on aching breast,
When home, where truest love can reign,
Receives its severed ones again.
So, when the toil of life is o'er,
Comes happy rest for evermore,
Where pilgrims from the world's highway
Rejoice in God's dear home for aye.

MANY a sky of summer blue
The shepherd's humble cottage knew,
Many a firelight's ruddy glow
Flicker'd o'er the winter's snow.
Swallows built beneath its eaves,
Springtide deck'd its walls with leaves,
Seasons brought no anxious care,
Calm content was nestled there.
Round it odours stole from flowers,
O'er it oaks entangled bowers,
Butterflies, in sunny ray,
Came, on painted wing, to play ;
From its doorway stretch'd a scene
Beauteous in the summer sheen.

Like a sentinel the while
Yonder stood the stately pile,
Where the lords had liv'd and died—
Owners of those acres wide.
Intervening grassy downs,
Gemm'd by daisies' floral crowns,
Gave a place where flocks might stray,
Where their frolics lambs might play ;

Dog and shepherd linger'd near—
This their happy working sphere.

When the rooks in straggling line
Sought their home at day's decline,
Homeward too the shepherd sped,
Where the gentle housewife spread
Frugal meal, while welcome best
Sooth'd the weary one to rest.
Ralph, a boy of promise rare,
Is the shepherd's joy and care.
Only child, for him he lives,
Burning love the mother gives ;
Both for him toil day by day
Hoarded wealth to store away.
Mingled beauty in their boy
Could not but be source of joy.
When he stood by river brim,
Glowing after lengthen'd swim,
Classic art could scarce compare
With the beauty figur'd there—
Features artists love to trace,
Chestnut hair, a ruddy face,
Eyes that beam'd intelligence,
Readiness in every sense !

Oft the tutor from the Hall
At the cottage made a call,
Pleas'd that Ralph's inquiring mind
Sought from him fresh lore to find.
Constant intercourse thus rose,

3

Progress mark'd each study's close,
Good success full well repaid
Efforts by the tutor made ;
Till, by means of hoarded store,
Ralph stepp'd from his cottage door,
Seeking still to reach the light
Crowning wisdom's giddy height.

Gloom fell on the cottage floor,
Light seem'd banish'd evermore ;
Long the night and dull the day
Now that Ralph had gone away.
Yet to parents' heart what joy
Was a letter from their boy !
Read, re-read, 'mid smiles and tears,
Echo'd in the neighbours' ears ;
Till, from many a letter sent,
Loving hearts were made content,
Joyful that their boy's success
Came the toil of years to bless.

Varying years their course had run,
Shepherd's work was well-nigh done,
Darksome grief's relentless storm
More than age had bow'd his form.
Yet on mossy bank he took
Wonted place beside the brook,
Though his faltering step was slow,
Though his voice was weak and low,
Though the heart-pains furrows trac'd,
And the sunny smiles effac'd.

Seated in the cottage shade,
Now no more her heaven made,
'Neath the sorrow's gloomy cloud,
Was the old wife's figure bow'd,
Craving, as her only joy,
Tidings from her absent boy.

Ralph, by work of able brain,
Rose in legal lore to gain
Place of honour and renown.
Wealth for him threw garlands down,
Great ones treated him as kin,
Crowds his flowing words took in,
Cheers his burning utterance fann'd,
High-born ladies sought his hand !
Place and power now turn'd his head,
Pomp and gold ambition fed ;
Deep down in his harden'd heart
Pride conceal'd its venom'd dart ;
All the love of former days
Languish'd in good fortune's rays ;
He his origin disclaim'd,
Never loving parents nam'd,
And the life of days obscure
As a secret kept secure.

When the spring its fragrance shed
Ralph across the ocean sped,
Basking on a foreign shore,
Happy in his money'd store,
Never caring for the smart

Paining e'er his mother's heart.
Yet, divorc'd from charity,
Wealth is gilded misery,—
Sordid passions round it cling,
Till it flies on rapid wing.
From the land long left behind,
Swifter than the course of wind,
Full of ill the message flash'd,
Golden cup to earth it dashed ;
Failure, startling all the world,
Down the golden idol hurl'd,
And the man who scorn'd the poor
Was as beggar on the moor,
Was as poor as shepherd old
Feebly watching by the fold !

Friends of sunshine turn'd to stone,
Hearts that fawn'd now ceas'd to own.
Like the prodigal Ralph wept,
In his soul the warm life crept,
Love of home again return'd,
Mother's love within him burn'd,
Urging swift amends to make,
Home his broken heart to take,
There to soothe parental fears,
And bewail the past in tears.

Eventide had come again,
Childhood's chimes rang out in pain,
Rooks the same old journey made
Back to elm-trees' nightly shade ;

While before the cottage door
Unknown children scamper'd o'er
What was once his own domain—
Would those days were back again !

" Want the shepherd ?   Ah, too late !
Yesterday the churchyard gate
Open'd for his funeral train—
He returns not here again ! "
" Where's his wife ?   Why months ago
She too pass'd from life of woe,
Vainly longing for the bliss
Yielded by one loving kiss
From a dear one far away,
Lost upon the world's highway ! "

Kneeling by a new-made mound
In the churchyard's holy ground
Was a stranger bow'd in grief ;
Tears for him gave no relief,
Sorrow's cry from that lich gate
Only echo'd, " Late ! Too late ! "

TEARS.

Poor emblems of a broken heart
   From anguish fountains sent,
When sorrows deep sad vigils keep
   And days of joy are spent !

Weep on, poor heart, till on the cloud
   The rainbow's radiant form
Reveals the love that glows above
   The blackness of the storm.

Weep on—the Man of Sorrows wept
   Beneath the morning beam,
Where olives threw their sombre hue
   O'er Cedron's winding stream ;

While yonder stood Jerusalem,
   Majestic as of old,
And heaven's bright light danc'd on the height
   Where shone the Temple's gold.

Weep on, as He wept 'mid the graves
   Where Lazarus soundly slept ;
He drank each woe thy heart can know,
   For thee has " Jesus wept."

He comes in tender love to mark
  Each tear-drop in life's cup,
To soothe each grief and in relief
  The broken heart bind up.

He waits to comfort stricken hearts,
  And leads by precious grace
To that fair shore where never more
  Shall anguish tears have place.

ALONE.

ALL thoughts will dwell on thee, Jemmie,
  When thou art far away ;
And all my hopes will be, Jemmie,
  For thy returning day.

Without thee home can be no home,
  Each day will be a year,
And every dream of restless sleep
  Will bring my darling near.

Oh, joy beyond all telling,
  When voyages are o'er,
And thou in happy home, Jemmie,
  Shalt leave me nevermore.

Then speed thee back to me, Jemmie,
  Good angels guard thee well ;
And love and peace unite, Jemmie,
  To cast o'er thee a spell.

And when the storm-blast howls, Jemmie,
  Across the surging sea ;
My constant prayers shall rise, Jemmie,
  That God may succour thee.

My full heart goes with thee, Jemmie,
   With thee alone to dwell ;
And love, unchanging love, Jemmie,
   Breathes in my last farewell.

No news ! and yet I strive each weary day
The best to hope for, as I try to say,
" Thy will be done." He'll surely come home soon,
For Heaven will grant me this my dearest boon !
And yet alone from day to day I wait,
And start in hope if winds but shake the gate ;
Upon the road I fix my aching eyes,
Anon hope lives, and then again it dies ;
I hie me to the crowd upon the pier,
As vessel after vessel cometh near,
But Jemmie's ship comes not to cheer my heart
And bid its dark forebodings all depart.
O God, in mercy hearken to my plea,
Bring back again my dear one on the sea ;
Oh, give me patience to await Thy while,
Then crown that patience with his loving smile !

   I've waited long alone, Jemmie,
      Since last I saw thy face ;
   I've waited all in vain for thee
      To take the vacant place ;

   And sorrow's cloud keeps daylight from
      The window of my heart,
   And gloomy grief can ne'er again
      From that dark chamber part.

Hope linger'd on in fitful gleams
  From weary day to day,
But fail'd at last, as taper light
  That flickering dies away.

I wander by the sea, Jemmie,
  And find each rolling wave
Brings me a message of a love
  Deep down in ocean grave.

Sometimes the wild sea's song, Jemmie,
  Is mournful dirge for thee ;
Sometimes I hear a solemn knell
  That rings across the sea.

And when the storm-clouds rise, Jemmie,
  And waves in tempest roar,
And for their loved ones on the sea
  Hearts tremble on the shore—

'Tis then I feel that thou, Jemmie,
  Art near me once again,
To soothe my life of sorrow deep
  And ease my heart of pain ;

To whisper of the coming day
  When joy shall crown each head,
When graves the lost of earth restore
  And seas release their dead ;

When there shall be no sea, Jemmie,
  And all the good are blest ;
Where the wicked cease from troubling
  And the weary are at rest.

THE CHURCHYARD.

FAR stretch'd the scene o'er pleasant hill and dale,
Bright shone the sun upon the flow'ry vale,
Loud sang the birds from many a leafy spray,
The little brook made music on its way,
The zephyrs, from the ocean passing by,
Through green woods flitted with a gentle sigh ;
While larks' sweet notes resounded far and near,
And merry ploughboys' songs fell on the ear :
This was a springtide scene.

       I came once more.
A russet tint had cloth'd the landscape o'er,
The swallows were returning back again
To sunny homes beyond the azure main,
The birds forgot to warble merry lay,
The brook, now full, made melancholy way,
And cold blasts rushing through the forest shade
The leaves of autumn scatter'd in the glade.

I came again. Rude winds were echoing round,
An icy chain the silenc'd brook had bound.
'Twas now a village church first met my gaze,
Illumin'd by the sun's scant winter rays.
All summer hid from view by leafy trees,
Unknown it stood, save as the gentle breeze

Sweet bore its chiming music on the air
To call the villagers to daily prayer.
I wander'd to the spot with stricken soul,
And prayed that patience might the thoughts
    control.
Around the little church the churchyard lay—
To me a hopeless scene of dread decay.
The fleecy snow spread over every mound,
And crested all the gravestones of the ground.

An infant here had found a dismal bed,
There slept a youth among the unknown dead,
An uncouth stone mark'd out the old man's grave,
And where the winds made coarser grasses wave
Slept one forgotten long, and long unknown,
For age had crumbled e'en the very stone,
Perchance by love erected, wet with tears,
To speak (how vain the hope !) for many years !
'Twas here I musing stood and well-nigh wept,
Depress'd to think of those who round me slept ;
Too blind to gaze where holy spirits soar
And drink in light on light for evermore,
Till God Himself in Beatific Light
Reveals all glory to the ravish'd sight.
I mov'd away in haste and pass'd a mound
That tore the verdure's carpet spread around,
And marked a grave that yawn'd amid the gloom
To seize its own, and hold till day of doom.
To lich-gate, priest and choir with Holy Sign
For funeral rites had pass'd in solemn line,
As onward mov'd a white-rob'd maiden train,

Whose voices mingled in a minor strain,
As round the dead they sang the sweet refrain—

" Far spent the hours of night,
    The day draws near,
In which in raiment white
    The Saints appear.

Our lov'd ones in their rest
    Of Paradise
Await the morning blest
    When they shall rise.

Could we the chorus hear,
    The glory see,
Where death and sorrow's tear
    Can never be,

Where angels gather round
    On pinions bright,
And evermore resound
    The songs of light.

Could we the mists remove
    That veil from sight
The joys of Beatific Love
    And fadeless light,

Then would our longing prayer
    Speed on the day
Which breaks when sin and care
    All flee away—

The prayer that perfect bliss
    For faithful dead
May at that morning's kiss
    On each be shed.

Frail body, here we leave
    In holy rest,
Till Jesus shall receive
    His children blest."

The song seem'd endless lullaby to me,
And earthward eyes no ray of hope could see.

In rapid flight the course of time pass'd round,
And once again I stood on holy ground.
'Twas when the springtide's new-made garment
    green
Had mantled softly o'er the laughing scene.
Its verdure bright and tuneful birds the while
Had caus'd e'en churchyard gloom to bear a
    smile.
Beneath the solemn yew's more solemn shade
By sleeping dust, where love's last offerings fade,
I pensive sat, and soon the mists of sleep
Strove from my mind earth's troubled scene to
    keep.
In vain they fell, for then a passing dream
Brought back again the subject of my theme.
Methought a child wove in the sunny hours,
To deck a grassy mound, a cross of flowers,
And sitting there the guard of sleeping dust
She rais'd a song that warbled hope and trust—

" Safe from the storms of earth,
　All sorrow pass'd away,
God grant thee His dear rest
Till comes the morning blest
　Of endless day.

Time ends ! the angel's call
　Shall bid thee joyful rise,
And saints in glory bright
Shall in all bliss unite
　Above the skies.

For winter gloom shall pass
　When comes the sunlit day,
And everlasting spring
Shall bid the ransom'd sing
　The victor's lay."

Thus clos'd the song ! Dark vapours hung around,
Deep silence swallow'd up each 'livening sound,
All nature throbb'd in pain and strove to die,
And beauty spread its wings from earth to fly !
'Twas then burst forth a full red fiery sun,
E'en such as bids farewell when day is done,
And from the east slow broke the mists away,
Rich tinted by the sun's deep crimson ray,
From earth in varied tints fair flowers upsprang ;
Then trumpet's blare throughout Creation rang,
And echo'd in the deepest caves below ;
It made the sun unheard-of glory show,
And call'd from dust of earth and ocean's bed

The countless multitudes of holy dead.
Then burst such glory that the glorious sun
To it was dark ; a loud song was begun
As in His glory, passing to His throne,
The King of Saints gave welcome to His own.
I saw the sons of light in glory stand,
I watch'd the throng pass on to glory's land,
I listen'd as with angel hosts they sang,
And woke as heaven-born echoes round me rang.
And now I know our happy dead will wake,
Each spirit shall its glorious body take,
Our lov'd ones, mourn'd, the new world shall
    restore,
That we and they may part again no more.
Be brave, sad heart, leave thy dear dead to rest,
In Christ, Who rose, the sleeping dead are blest

VENGEANCE.

LIT by the moonbeam,
   Trembling ever,
On the murmuring stream,
   Murmuring ever ;
Wrapt in midnight sleep,
Calm in silence deep,
Where had been known to weep
  Wounded hearts never—
There in the flow'ry glade,
Resting in leafy shade,
Blest with a moonbeam's kiss
Stood Amy's home of bliss !

Around its hearth a happy circle met,
Upon its glow no cloud of sorrow yet
Had planted gloomy shadow as a spell
To break the charms that came in joy to dwell.
A noble brother was its cherish'd hope,
And nobly he with tempting foes would cope,
Or boldly grapple lurking danger's hand
That menaced happy home and fatherland.
For him the homestead yielded best of pleasure,
His heart held Amy as its priceless treasure,
And all its sunshine in the merry while
Was gather'd from her ready, winsome smile !

4

Far westward fell the fading ray,
That told the day had fled away ;
The zephyrs o'er the hamlet stray'd,
Scarce mov'd the leaflets in the glade,
The woodland vespers usher'd night,
The taper stars gave twinkling light,
As nightingales poured forth a song
Where babbling streamlets rush'd along.

There in the twilight,
   Tearfully, sadly,
Shrinking from sunlight,
   Wringing hands madly,
Wander'd a beauteous maid
On to the churchyard's glade,
   There to stay and weep,
   Sad vigils long to keep,
   Where the dead ever sleep
   Under the greensward deep !
She sadly by the sacred fabric stay'd,
And fervently with heart of anguish pray'd.
Yet wild her look as by that grave she knelt,
No meaning had the theme on which she dwelt.
She mingled broken prayers and holy song
With cries, that echo sadly bore along,
For vengeance on an unknown head to fall,
And for herself relief in death's enthrall.
" Amy ! Amy ! What dost thou here alone,
In tears still lingering by the sculptured stone ?
Why vigils keep beside the buried dead ?
Hope has not taken wings and from us fled ! "

" No ! no ! but Harry comes not, so I wait
A weary while within the churchyard gate,—
He'll come ! "—the thought mad laughter calls,
And echo laughs again from sacred walls.

The cowering pall of night grows light and lighter
    still
As solemn orb of night slow rises o'er the hill ;
A silvery beam across the landscape steals,
And churchyard relics night no more conceals.
        There in the moonlight,
        Crouching in dewy night,
        Amy in anguish lies,
        Bearing heart agonies.
  " When will Harry bid me share
  Home's delight and pleasures, where
  He awaits the perfect day,
  Where for us our dear ones pray?
  Oh ! my heart must burst in pain
  Till I see my lov'd again !
  List ! his voice once more I hear,
  As it calls dies out my fear !
  Eyes grow dim, yet I've his hand !
  Who are they that by me stand ?
What thrilling senses soul and body fill !
There's bliss in dying ;—Harry loves me still ! "

The wind loud howls and dark, dark is the night,
Deep thunder rolls, and fearful flashing light
Divides the pall of clouds that hide the heaven,
As earth to all the tempest's rage is given !

It is a time when guilty conscience wakes,
And of the past a dreaded picture makes !
Amid the storm the exile murderer sleeps,
Yet 'tis a sleepless sleep, in which he weeps,
And, restless, ever rolls his throbbing head,
And starts in visions of the murder'd dead !
In dreams he sees again his victim die,
He hears the curse of Cain pierce from the sky,
Cold sweats stand on him, as again is seen,
In solemn grandeur, 'neath the silver sheen
The churchyard, where, in shapeless dust, we lay
(Till comes the morn of resurrection day)
The ruins of the temple of the soul,
That flits from earth, and from the earth's control.
The night is still, the owl is heard alone
To screech around the churchyard's crumbling
    stone,
As from her place beside a new-made grave
He hears once more the shriek that Amy gave
As Harry fell.   In vain he strives to turn
From eyes that fiercely in his bosom burn.
He hears the curse, " What peace, what peace
    hast thou ?
Revenge shall follow thee till thou shalt bow
Beneath its fiery yoke ; and conscience chains
Shall ever find new links of gnawing pains
In woes more woeful than the tongue can tell,
Till Harry's blood has dragged thee down to hell ! "
" Forbear ! forbear ! " the gasping exile cries,—
A dismal thunder-peal alone replies,
The lightning-flash, amid his ruin'd shed,
Had left the unknown murderer with the dead !

REST.

When the twilight hour is near,
When slow forms the dewy tear,
When the flitting bats appear,
        And flow'rets sleep ;
When the evening hues invest
All the crimson-tinted west,
Calling May-flies from their rest
        Till starlets peep ;
When the blackbird's sweet "good-night"
Echoes to the dying light,   ♥
When the owl begins his flight
        On noiseless wing;
When the vesper bell is rung,
When the work of day is done,
Evensong is sweetly sung
        Its peace to bring ;
Then, when worldly turmoil ends,
When the toil-worn homeward wends,
Where the love-look welcome sends,
        How sweet the rest !

When the Sunday bells are rung,
When the Eucharist is sung,.
And the joyous thankful tongue
        Finds music best ;

When, as Moses struck of old
Rock that living streams unroll'd,
Sunday strikes toil's rock of gold
                For rest to spring
Then the weary worker knows
Joy from holy rest that flows
As his grateful anthem shows
                How hearts can sing.
And when life's strange journey's o'er,
When is reached the peaceful shore
Where can weigh down never more
                This earth's unrest,
Comes a rest without a sigh—
Rest, no tear to dim the eye—
Rest, with angel's lullaby,
                For ever blest !

CONTRASTS.

WITHIN, the blazing logs gave dancing light,
  Rich hangings caught its glare,
Which bade defiance to the outer night,
  And banish'd restless care,—
Snug comfort brooded with his downy wing
And taught the song the cricket loves to sing.

Without, the howling wind like beast of prey
  Woke sleeping childhood's fear,
A blinding sleet fell on the traveller's way,
  Leaves rustled dead and sear ;
The search for shelter and repose was vain,
And hope had roll'd away with Charles's wain.

  . . . . . .

Within, disconsolate, a weeping maid
  Bewail'd the bitter fate
Of broken word and faithless vows once made,
  And love that turn'd to hate,
Nor tears nor sighs could heal the sorrow's smart
Of love uprooted from the inmost heart.

Without, the newly wed left church porch grey,
  The bells with joy were mad,
The children's flow'rets scattered bridal way,
  And ev'ry soul was glad,—

Blue sky and golden sunshine promis'd store
Of brimming happiness for evermore.

.   .   .   .   .   .

Within, the windows veil'd and silence deep,
    The scent of fading flowers,
A stiffen'd form embrac'd by chilly sleep,
    While through the tearful hours
The watchers, as the taper's light burnt dim,
Recited holy prayer and requiem hymn.

Without, the happy shout of boyhood's mirth,
    The birds that ever sing,
The sunlight bidding all the waking earth
    A scented garland bring,
Recalling life to revel in its glare
And raise a song of rapture everywhere.

.   .   .   .   .   .

Below, the journey up the rugged height,
    The conflict with the foe,
The mists that keep us from the light
    As doubts flit to and fro ;
Heartaches and sorrows crowding all the day,
And tempting music luring from the way.

Above, the rest, where only rest has place,
    The sword exchang'd for palm,
Revealèd glory from the Father's Face,
    The shout of triumph psalm,
Where none can suffer and where none can die,
For ever banish'd sorrow, tear and sigh.

SACRED ECHOES.

Upon the abbey pavement old
  The evening rays were pour'd,
And on it brush of sunset gold
  West window's glories stor'd.

Till slowly twilight's softer ray
  Subdued the richer light,
And in recesses darkness lay
  To beckon on the night.

And shades of monument and tomb
  Pass'd as the daylight died,
And lost themselves in deepening gloom
  Befitting eventide.

Yet still a mystic twilight fell
  Within the choir's far height,
Where incense mists rose as a spell
  To weave the robe of night.

And piercing it the songs of praise
  Re-echo'd to the sky,
And holy chants the faithful raise
  Were wafted up on high—

The music that from days of old
  Has e'er to God been given—
The wings that lift frail man to hold
  Communion sweet with heaven !

But where the voices loud with joy
  At th' Consecration feast—
And where each white-rob'd singing boy,
  And ministering priest ?

Not silent in the grave's embrace,
  Not hush'd, for still they sing—
Sweet echoes from their resting-place
  The songs of Zion bring.

And through the many changeful years
  That since have pass'd away,
Have faithful hearts sung on in tears
  The songs of golden day.

Yet still within the ancient pile
  Methinks their vocal strain
Pours forth in sweetness to beguile
  The hearts that beat in pain.

The sacred walls yet bear along
  The solemn chant and sweet,
And past and present join in song
  And anthem's joys repeat.

But echoes from the music clear
  Of voice we may not hear,
From choir to nave, now far, now near,
  Fall softly on the ear.

They make me glad, and yet I weep
  As falls their cadence sweet,
For ever vigils must I keep
  Till I the singer meet,

Where faultless choirs for aye unite
  No faltering songs to raise,
Where children of eternal light
  Ne'er weary in their praise.

When comes each day the white-rob'd train
  With solemn step, and slow,
And slowly to the organ's strain
  The priests and choir-throng go.

Then when their moving harmony
  The echoes onward bear,
That voice inspiring ecstasy
  We feel is wanting there.

For he, our boy, of beauty rare
  With love-light in his eyes,
No more will pray a choir-boy's prayer,
  No more in song uprise.

But when the Abbey service ends
　　And angels watch around,
The voice we lov'd again ascends
　　And soothing notes abound.

"We pray Thee help Thy servant whom
　　With Thy most precious Blood
Thou hast redeem'd"—this from his room
　　Oft wafted up to God.

This was his last-sung prayer below,
　　God's angels did him throng,
And bore to Paradise we know
　　The singer and the song.

And then within the Abbey-ground,
　　While sorrow bow'd each head,
His choral brethren standing round
　　Sang service of the dead.

And there we left him, lov'd and blest,
　　Asleep in grassy grave ;
A white cross marks that place of rest
　　And flow'rets round it wave ;

And ever round that little bed
　　The echoes never cease
To roll the anthems for the dead
　　And tell of endless peace.

NO MARRIAGE BELLS TO-DAY.

February 27, 1892, the date fixed for the wedding of Prince Albert Victor, who died January 14, 1892.—R.I.P.

HOPE made a posy rich and rare
    A loving bridal gift to be,
    A promise of felicity
    And changeless love in high degree,
For loving hearts to share.

Alas! the flowers of bridal cheer
    Bedew'd in bitter tears must die,
    Exhaling still a fragrant sigh
    E'en as in sympathy they lie—
A wreath beside the bier.

Hope rang in joy a marriage peal,
    From England's towers grey and old,
    A nation's joy the music told,
    O'er city, hamlet, vale and wold—
A song of lasting weal.

Alas! Alas! for human bliss
    Grief's spectre hushed the merry clang,
    A mournful peal in sorrow rang,
    A requiem the mourners sang—
Death stole the bridegroom's kiss.

Hope, in a chorus love had blent,
 Sent forth a gladsome nuptial song,
 The echoes bore its waves along,
 And organ's diapasons strong
Harmoniously were lent.

But hope's bright music died away !
 Adown the church's sacred fold
 The tones of Dies Iræ roll'd,
 In chilling breath the Dead March told
How death held icy sway.

Yet hope fails not where faith is high ;
 Love's cherish'd blossom never dies,
 Eternal springtide's flow'rets rise,
 The joy-bells ring o'er Paradise
And angels linger by.

Soon shall the marriage feast be spread,
 The Bride—the Church—in fair array,
 In splendour of th' eternal day
 Shall own the Bridegroom's smile alway
When God recalls the dead. .

MY BOYS AND I.

WHEN the days are dark and dreary,
When the lagging hours are weary,
Then to cheer with life's young dream
Bid my boys around me beam.

When the summer sunlight glances,
And the heart in gladness dances,
Let young life enhance the bliss,
And on beauty plant its kiss.

When the cup of joy is sweetest,
And the rapid hours are fleetest,
Sweeter will the chalice be
If my loved ones drink with me.

When the step is light and airy,
Leading on through landscapes fairy,
Joyous youth with artless air
Must with me the journey share.

When the Christmas brings its greeting,
And the scatter'd friends are meeting,
Half its joy will disappear
If I have no young friends near.

When another year is ending,
Friends in love good wishes sending,
Best of all, my boys' good cheer,
Wishing me a glad New Year.

Summer days with them are brighter,
Winter days with them grow lighter,
Landscapes fair are yet more fair,
When the young life frolics there.

When the clouds the light are hiding,
Sorrow in the heart abiding,
Youthful love for me will form
Rainbow's arch on cloud of storm.

When the light around is paling,
When the powers of life are failing,
Youthful music pour'd amain
Then shall make me young again.

Thus, though days be dull or cheery,
Whether hours be swift or weary,
Boyhood's love still lingering near
Gives me sunshine all the year.

THE AFTER-DAYS.

To F. W.

ASCENSION DAY ! and all the bells had rung,
And triumph music o'er the city flung;
Communions had been made, and cherish'd hearts
Were knit with us in Him Who earth departs
To be through all the Church the Food and Life—
The Strength in all the toil of earthly strife.
Then far away, the smoky town forgot,
We wander'd where the blue forget-me-not
Had fring'd the widening river, where the trees,
Fresh budded, murmur'd to the passing breeze,
And, arching o'er the water's sedgy side,
Droop'd low to kiss the river's brimming tide.
We row'd in glee beneath the sunlit sky,
And boys' sweet voices and the larks' on high
Went mingled through the realms of azure state,
As incense up to heaven's golden gate.
And now in after-days comes back again
The music of the song in sweet refrain,
And once again the river scene is here
With laughing spring dear memory's course to
    cheer.
Oh ! in the after-days for us in store
God grant the same dear ones may sing once
    more

Where life's clear river flows through ageless
    bowers,
And endless springtide yields its fadeless flowers.

'Twas Christmas Eve, and one we lov'd[1] was dead,
The Holy Child had bid Death's angel spread
His pinions, bearing hence from winter's snow,
From nipping frosts and chilly winds that blow,
The dear one early called the cross to bear,
That earlier he the crown of life might wear.
And when the shadows of the dying year
Lay darkly o'er the woodland dead and sear
With holy songs we laid him to his rest,
And left him sleeping sound on Jesus' breast.
And now in after-days, the love not less,
The memory of his gentle love we bless.
Oh ! in the after-days when life is spent
And endless Easter follows life's long Lent,
God grant we meet again in joyous band
Where deathless glory fills Emmanuel's land.

Year after year, as summer days come round,
To country home,[2] where health and rest are found,
Comes youthful life to make the woodland ring
In union with the harmonies that spring   ·
From village bells, from ever-flowing streams
And song of birds awoke by morning beams.
Here graceful forms that mock the sculptor's skill,
In limpid stream may lave and sport at will ;

    [1] I. E., *obit.* 1875, aged 15.
    [2] F. W.'s country place in Hertfordshire.

Here boyhood's glee dispels the wearing care,
And gloomy thought is driven from his lair.
Then, when the busy joy of day is o'er,
The place of prayer is sought, and blessings pour
To shield from harm the hours of guileless sleep,
When guardian angels faithful vigils keep,
Till song of birds awakes another day—
A summer day too soon to pass away.
And in the after-days those sunshine hours
Give light to tint each darksome cloud that lowers ;
Oh ! in the after-days for which we yearn,
The visions blest may all our lov'd discern
In home of endless sunshine, where shall be
No farewell word, and no dividing sea.

THE LAY BROTHER.

HEART music ever in him rose
From matin hour till day's repose—
Music chastening earthly woes.

The world and self were set aside
For love of Him, the Crucified,
And God in all was glorified.

Before the call of matin bell
The brother knelt within his cell,
As from his lips the utterance fell,

" Dear Lord, I fain would follow Thee,
Yet in the path laid out for me
No shadow of Thy Cross I see ;

To Thee in vow I pledge my life,
Can it be Thine with pleasure rife,
And nothing known of sorrow's strife ?

Yet in submission would I pray,
Lead as Thou wilt, be Thou my stay
Till ends the night in perfect day."

Next morn, before the Altar Shrine,
Where gleam'd aloft the Holy Sign,
Love drank in Love in Food Divine.

When fading tints were lingering still
Above the distant purple hill,
And song of birds had ceas'd to trill,

One, plague-struck, bending 'neath his fate,
With scarcely strength enough to wait
Till willing hands could ope the gate,

Was given to that brother's care
To tend and nurse, as rose the prayer
For grace his brethren's griefs to share.

'Twas but a youth with pallid face
And features cast with beauty's grace,
A stripling in life's chequer'd race.

The brother sat beside the bed,
His hand was cool on fever'd head,
His glance a constant solace shed.

But ere the morning gave its glow,
As night's faint taper burnèd low
And embers scarce a spark could show,

On rapid wing the angels sped
And flutter'd round the narrow bed—
The stranger in the cell lay dead.

The brother clos'd the filmèd eyes,
His prayer of love pierc'd leaden skies
That both might meet in Paradise.

And ere the nightfall came again
Contagious plague enlarged its reign,
The brother lay in mortal pain.

Two dead ones in the cell at rest,
Asleep, with hands cross'd on the breast,
By ne'er a fitful dream oppress'd.

A voice from thence rings ceaselessly,
" Thy deeds of precious charity
To these the least are done to Me."

THE HOLLY TREE.

I LOVE the legendary lore,
With hidden truths, a goodly store,
That soothe us in the weary strife
And gladden in the toil of life.
Dear Holly Tree—the *Holy* Tree—
Hast thou a legend got for me ?

Ah ! thorns first came with sin of man
And fairest of earth's scenes o'erran.
Then first earth's pleasures prov'd a snare
And all earth's treasures anxious care ;
The pleasures left but anguish sore,
And treasures could not peace restore ;
Earth's joys proved false, and Heaven's
      fair light
Seem'd lost in everlasting night.
Then One in tenderest love drew near,
Earth's heavy-laden sons to cheer,
To stay the march of sin's foul train
And open Paradise again.
For this He bore the Cross, the scorn,
The mocking robe, the crown of thorn,
The bitter death, that men might live
The life the God-Man came to give.

Urged on by love's undying flame,
Unmov'd by taunts, S. Joseph came,
The Body of his Lord to crave
And rest It in his own new grave.
And He, Who had no place of rest,
As o'er earth's wilderness He press'd,
Found rest where fragrant flowers bloom,
Found rest but in another's tomb !
One relic Joseph bears away—
The Crown of Thorns—to tell for aye
That thorny crown wins crown of gold
For soldiers in the conflict bold.

Long years succeed.   The faithful band
Uprear the Cross in many a land,
And Joseph to our England came
First herald of the Saving Name—
Still cherishing the Crown of pain
All dyed with precious crimson stain.
A part made Glastonbury's Thorn—
To bloom when comes the Christmas morn—
And lo ! the rest was seen to grow
With leaves of memory—e'er to show
Again the thorns of agony
That pierced our Lord on Calvary—
With berries red, like drops of blood
That fell for us from Holy Rood,
Bespeaking love of Him Who died—
The love of Jesus Crucified.

JOAN OF ARC.

THE foes advanc'd, and Victory sat and smiled
Upon their arms! The old man and the child
Alike in terror, trembling, quailed. Advance!
And on they make through fairest part of France
A bloody way. Stern desolation set
His chilling hand on all, gaunt famine ate
The plenty up, and towns like Vulcan's height
Alarms gave forth, and awful made the night
With cruel flames that bended to the wind
As clouds of smoke came rolling up behind!
Are these war's glories? Where the hum of life
That mingled when the mirthful song was rife?—
A moaning only left, or silence drear!
Where stand the promises of Autumn's cheer?—
All trampled out in war's red barrenness—
Naught now remains the labourer's toil to bless!
Where happy homesteads stood with joy replete,
Where old familiar friends were wont to greet
Each other with a smile and kindly word,
And chat the while on all that each had heard,
Naught meets the gazer's ever tearful eye
Save ruins, from whose embers rolls on high
In heavy pillars, peaceful twilight's shroud,
The far-extending, smoky 'whelming cloud.

73

Distressèd country ! Is there none for thee
Will brave the fight and strive to set thee free
From inroads of th' ambitious English foe,
Regain his conquests, and at once o'erthrow
The schemes, hell-born, of those who boldly stand
To curse with havoc home and fatherland ?
Yea ; one comes forward, though unskilled in arms,
Untried in battle-field and war's alarms.
A simple village maid, who o'er and o'er
In anguish heard the tales the travellers bore,
And musing wished that she could take command,
Will save her people and her native land.
Is she deceived ? Can earthly ears receive
A mystic message heavenly voices weave ?
Can earthly eyes drink in—no earth between—
The glowing splendours of the heavenly scene ?
I cannot say—but faith in her was strong—
The pure in heart can hear the angels' song—
And in the song she knew a charge from heaven
To save her trembling blood-stained land was
      given.
While holy angels round her vigils kept
And visions solaced as she guileless slept,
Strange voices bade her drive beyond the coast
The legions of the dread invading host,
Assured that she to Rheims her prince should bring
And there behold him crown'd her country's king.

'Twas time to stir ! Town after town was lost,
The foe victorious had to Orleans cross'd—
The only stronghold left, whose guarded tower

Bore flag of Charles before proud England's
    power,—
'Twas doomed to be for Henry's wolves a prey
As succours fail'd, and hopes all died away.
Not so ; the Maid's brave heart must act its part.
In arms she comes, to bid the woes depart
From stricken France. Her words all hearts in-
    spire,
And courage flames from utterances of fire—

" At Heaven's behest, before my liege I stand,
The champion of our terror-stricken land.
I come, like one of old, in God's great Name
To bring the pride of cruel foes to shame,
And as the sling and stone avenged the wrongs,
And gave to Israel joy of triumph songs,
So I, with virgin sword, will rescue France,
And give the time for song and pipe and dance.
What though the lustre fades from out thy crown !
What though thy country be now trodden down !
With aid of saints and angels my weak hand
Can tear the shroud of sorrow from our land.
What though the foe would mount thy legal throne,
And claim the best of all we call our own !
By God's dear grace I'll turn the ebbing tide
Till flowing victory be on our side.
Arouse ye ! Follow me ! It is decreed
That France from England's grasp shall now be
    freed ;
Heaven's warrior hosts are with us for the right,
And Orleans shall be saved by ghostly might.

To arms ! With faith in God and hearts of steel,
Our sturdy ranks our country's wounds shall heal !
Advance ! Anon Rheim's sacred bells shall ring
A welcome to thee, God's anointed king ! "

The maid advances—knight in very deed—
In armour clad, erect on prancing steed,
With glittering sword and banner white as snow,
As hope's fair star shines on in happy glow.
Full soon, against the sky's unvaried blue,
The siegèd towers of Orleans rise to view.
From English hearts the spirit of dismay,
With ruthless hand, all courage tears away,
They shrink before the maiden's eye of fire,
Before her ranks the coward troops retire !
They fly ! they fly ! France, tell it out in song !
Ye clanging bells, the triumph notes prolong !
Historic pages, tell in words of gold
How one, like faithful Deborah of old,
Has with the sword of God the foe o'erthrown—
Has led her king triumphant to his throne !
Ye surging crowds, send up the wild acclaim
In grateful homage to heroic name !

Her country free, her loving heart would fain
Find welcome rest in village home again.
The girlish loves and scenes, long left behind,
With all dear memories ever intertwined,
From feudal pomp and glittering state recall
To peaceful life within the cottage wall.
Not so ! Charles needs her service in the field,

Her cheering presence still will victory yield,
And she, reluctant, yet for fatherland
Consents again in battle ranks to stand—
Consents, though angels no commandment gave
And nightfall dreams be silent as the grave !

Hark !   Hear ye not the shout—the victors' cry ?
See, see, the stricken Frenchmen scattered fly !
Weep, gentle hearts, in bitter tears o'erflow
As skies grow dark and stars no longer glow,
For she, the purest heart of that rude age,
The worthiest patriot found in archives' page,
The faithful to her country, self, and God,
Is branded witch—too base to tread the sod—
Condemn'd as earth's offscouring, worse than vile,
To meet the witch's doom in flaming pile !
O God ! it cannot be !   Have men no heart ?
Have they in chivalry no longer part ?
Some hand perforce must stretch itself to save,
Some voice must ring back freedom for the brave !
Not one ?   O heavens, enshroud thy azure skies !
Thou sun, withdraw thy beams as from us flies
Dear Mercy's angel !   Trembling earth, proclaim
Anathema on blackest deed of shame !

Our warm hearts shrink from that last scene of all,
As she, the innocent, goes forth from prison wall
To meet dread death, undaunted as of yore
When in her hand the battle-flag she bore.
No murmuring word is wrung by anguish dire,
Heaven's solace grows in midst of rising fire,

Till her pure soul, in strength of Holy Name,
Elijah-like ascendeth in the flame
To see—not visions dim in air's dull space—
But glory's King revealèd face to face !

Know'st thou, O noble soul, in home above   ;
How men thy memory now revere and love,
Bewail thy fate and make thy name to be
A household word till dawn's eternity ?
It may be so.   And here 'tis ours to know
That heavenly gold is wrought in fire of woe,
That thy brief life of tribulation sore
Has work'd exceeding glory evermore,
Where earth's rejected, gaining life by loss,
Exchange for crown of gold the bitter cross.

WHEN THE DAY IS DONE.

LABOUR'S weary efforts end,
Hours of rest refreshment lend
As the dews of peace descend,
    When the day is done.

All the toiling of the way,
All the pain of troubled day,
All the cries of battle's fray
    End when day is done.

All home's dear ones fondly meet
Where the hearts in union beat,
As the happy moments fleet
    When the day is done.

When the shadow darkly lies,
When the teardrop dims the eyes,
Hope assures of Paradise,
    When life's day is done.

When temptations round us throng,
When the strife is fierce and long,
Faith bespeaks the victor's song
    When life's day is done.

When our dear ones droop and fade,
Lost awhile in death's deep shade,
Love tells love shall be repaid
    When life's day is done.

IN THE SNOW.

WHITHER away in the cold bleak air,
  As the snowflakes whiten the ground,
Cannot the wintry breezes scare,
  Or the darkness gathering round ?

Hinder me not, for, though old and grey,
  I must seek my Willie, my own ;
Out in the snow he roam'd away,
  And has left me all alone.

With a heart as chaste as the falling snow,
  And full of dear love to me,
He fondly yearns, I surely know,
  His mother again to see.

So on I go through the blinding snow,
  Not heeding the wrathful wind,
Out in the snow I fearless go
  My dearest, my own, to find.

Over him winds sang a lullaby low,
  The angel of snow linger'd near ;
Cloth'd in a garment whiter than snow
  Shall Willie, my own, appear.

6

For the snow-blasts open'd the pearly gates
   Of a city the purest see,
There my loved one watches and waits
   A welcome to give to me.

    .   .   .   .   .

Under a mound of the beautiful snow
   Slept a mother in sleep profound,
The boy of her love, lost long ago,
   In the beautiful snow she found.

MORNING.

From painted windows of the east,
   Bedeck'd with many a dewdrop gem,
   And crown'd with sunlit diadem,
   The Morn trips o'er the landscape's hem
To spread its golden feast.

The feather'd heralds of the bowers
   Expectant wait the leaves among
   To give in happiness a song
   Of truest welcome, loud and long,
That wakes the sleeping flowers.

He comes where hearts in anguish beat,
   Where sick men, tossing long in pain,
   Of weary lengthen'd night complain,
   And bids bright hope revive again
And gloomy shades retreat.

He flits across the resting-place
   Where slumber wraps the peaceful dead
   And smiles upon each sacred bed,
   Where daisy blossom lifts its head
The grassy mound to grace,

The promise of that day to give,
   When wrongs of earth shall be put right,
   Where gather not the mists of night,
   Where in the home of endless light
God's saints for ever live.

REPARATION.

The hunted fox secures a place of rest,
The birds aweary seek the hidden nest,
Yet for the Son of Man earth hath no bed—
No resting pillow for the throbbing Head.
To this His own created world He came,
And here His own revil'd His sacred Name,—
No room for Him in Bethl'hem's crowded inn,
The Light refused that kills the life of sin !
O shameful world ! Love rises in amends,
Her lavish gifts on Him ungrudging spends,
And rears the minster's vast entrancing pile—
A stony poem—breathing peace the while
The page of Time grows yellow with decay
And men in generations pass away.
For Him the wond'rous carving where no eye
Beholds the grace and beauty lost on high ;
For Him the cluster'd pillars rise afar,
Each mystic lamp hangs out its ruddy star,
The windows gleam, the gems like glow-worms
    shine ;
For Him the arts in harmony combine.
And He, Who is in truth the Living Bread,
In this our Bethlehem may rest His Head,
And with His lov'd ones evermore abide,
Till falls on life the peaceful eventide

That gathers God's elect from many lands,
And brings that temple near not made with hands.
About Him throng'd the sorrow-stricken folk,
From broken hearts the cry for healing broke,
And words of power absolved the sin-enchain'd,
And life and health the dead and sick regain'd,
And comfort dawn'd upon the heart of pain,
While childhood's peace came floating back again.
In doing good He made unceasing round
That ever consecrated Canaan's ground,
Yet earth for all return'd the bitter cry—
"Away with Him !   Away, and crucify !"
Ungrateful world !   The Church's songs arise,
Her children's Alleluias rend the skies ;
Her sweet Hosannahs blend in worship meet
With grateful hymns His Presence blest to greet,
In reparation for blaspheming jeer
And rabble-cry begetting cross and spear,
Till by that Cross and Passion men unite
With angels in the songs of endless light !

With jest profane, and many a ribald lay,
A frenzied mob crowds on the blood-stain'd way
Which leads to Golgotha, whose fetid air
Draws prowling night-beasts from the secret lair.
There on the bitter cross they lift Him high—
There, mocking, bow, and raise the taunting cry,
Till He, our Sacrifice, bows thorn-crown'd Head,
And for our life is number'd with the dead.
O Love, beyond the reach of words of love !
The theme of saints below and saints above !

What can we do but show our hearts' full store
In worship, highest, best, for evermore ?
They led Thee forth in mock procession's throng,
We in procession praise in triumph song,
With lifted banners speak the victory won,
The hosts of evil smitten and undone.
For parted garments,—we the frontal weave ;
For stench of death,—make censer's odours
  wreath ;
For darkness,—give the taper's soften'd light ;
For cross of shame,—erect in gem-set gold
Salvation's Sign—the badge of saints of old—
The crowning Sign—that throws its radiant glow
Where Cæsar's ruins crumble down below.
So will we worship, till, earth's mists dispell'd
And Schism's babel voices ever quell'd,
We in the great procession onward pass,
Where burning lamps shine on the sea of glass,
Where angels' censer yields the fragrant cloud,
And white-rob'd choristers of heaven aloud
Cry, " Honour, Glory, Blessing, Power, we give
To Him Who died and doth for ever live."

IN MEMORIAM, E. A. G.

STUDENT OF S. KATHARINE'S COLLEGE, TOTTENHAM.

Fell Asleep December 6, 1888.

On the eve of the Patron Saint,[1]
    As the year was dying away,
While the Advent shadows came creeping on,
    In the dull November day ;
The studies and books were laid aside,
The life had drawn to its eventide.

And the Priest, in the Altar's Rite,—
    In the last Communion of Love,—
Then gave to the dying the Bread of Life
    From the great High Priest above,
On Whose heart the gentle soul repos'd,
As on earthly things the eyelids clos'd.

On the Feast of the Sailor's Saint,[2]
    The mariner's toils were o'er,
She had pass'd the waves of this troublesome
       world,
    To rest on that peaceful shore
Where the waiting souls in the regions bright
Drink more and more of eternal light.

[1] S. Katharine.   [2] S. Nicholas.

In the Fane of the Holy Three,[1]
    'Neath Redemption's holy sign,
And before the Throne of the Virgins' Lord,
    Did we our dead resign,
With the prayer that she in the mansions fair
May more and more of God's visions share.

With the flowers we laid her to rest,
    As the day was dying away,
We said our " Good-bye " in the certain hope
    Of the Resurrection Day,
And a meeting blest, when our dear one wakes,
When the shadows flee and the morning breaks.

     [1] Church of the Holy Trinity, Stroud Green.

REMEMBRANCES.

LIFE's eventide draws near,
  Faint echoes play
In changeful music on the ear
  And die away ;
They bid youth's flow'rets bloom again,
And wavelets of a sweet refrain
Send back from many a bygone strain
  To cheer life's closing day.

The home where lov'd ones met
  Long, long ago,
In fancy's eye stands radiant yet
  In summer glow,
And voices death has hush'd awhile,
And faces lit with sunny smile,
Come back and lovingly beguile
  The days of winter snow.

The winding road of life
  In light and shade,·
Its weary way of toil and strife
  O'er hill and glade,
In sorrowing joy again we trace,
And fellow pilgrims in life's race
Once more beside us take a place
  As sunset colours fade.

When pilgrim days are o'er
    And conflicts end,
When love and glory evermore
    Harmonious blend,
Remembrances may add delight,
Where near and dear again unite,
Where grateful songs in God's own sight
    Eternally ascend.

EMIGRANTS.

THE lark o'erhead from morning grey
Had warbled loud a merry lay,
And sunshine with unstinted gleam
Had gilded mead and winding stream ;
Spring's glee attuned each subtle wire
Vibrating in fair Nature's lyre.
But deep below her festal song
The sad heart's minor notes may throng,
As shade of night deep down may be
Though sunlight dances on the sea,—
As dead leaves in the forest lie
Though bursting buds bring summer nigh.
And John, the farmer's man, was sad,
For things were strained and times were bad.
His lower'd wages, never high,
Could scarce the creature needs supply,
And that while in the far-off west
The virgin soil by labour dress'd
Was promising a bounteous yield
From many a waving harvest-field.

His Mary, wife for summers three,
Was loath to cross the mighty sea,
But scruples must be cast aside
If, waiting on the other side,

Success supplies with ready hand
The gifts withheld in fatherland.
Yet hope's bright music could not scare
The parting sorrow from its lair,
Nor still the heart's unbidden sigh
And clear the teardrop from the eye.
'Twas hard to leave each grassy mound
Where dear ones slept in holy ground;
A grief to leave the holy place
Where store of sacramental grace
Gave comfort in the daily strife
And strength to live the higher life;
Where round of festival and fast
Still knits the present with the past.
The broken words that said farewell,
The lingering looks o'er hill and dell,
Were all a bitterness and pain
Enough to tear the heart in twain.

Not much their store, but treasure best
Must journey with them to the West—
A book of prayer her mother gave,
A flow'ret from her baby's grave,
An ivy leaf from tower grey—
Memento of that parting day,
When, blessing them, the Rector's prayer
Commended them to God's dear care,—
A Bible,—with its yellow page
Recording length of pilgrimage
Of long-forgotten sire and dame
From whom he took unsullied name,—

And keepsakes giv'n with gen'rous hand
To cherish in the far-off land.

With heavy heart they left behind
Dear scenes of youth, old faces kind ;
They strained the eyes o'er woodland green
Where last the old church tower was seen ;
Their teardrops dimm'd the ocean's blue
As home's faint cloudland sank from view.
And many a day, as weary eyes
No prospect scann'd but sea and skies,
Those left at home would earnest pray
For dear ones sailing far away ;—
" Fair be the skies, the winds at peace,
From danger angels give release,
May heavenly guides the journey tend
And succour dear ones to the end ;
The good ship steer o'er trackless deep,
And God in love His children keep,
Give comfort in all toil and pain
And some day bring them home again."

Far in the land of woods and lakes
The emigrant his log home makes.
The earth, from patient toil each year,
In harvest gold gives hearty cheer,
While time with kindly hand effac'd
The deeper lines home-sickness trac'd.
Yet memory's faithful pencil drew
Undying pictures, ever new,
Of childhood's home, where each lov'd spot

Had rear'd its blue forget-me-not;
Of springtide scenes with sunny glow,
Of scented hawthorn's floral snow,
Of tender verdure where the cry,
Of " Cuckoo " echoed to the sky,
Of summer, brilliant as of yore,
With cottage garden's varied store,
Of autumn's fall with ruddy leaves
When swallows left the shelt'ring eaves,
And of the chilly winter days
When dancing light from ruddy blaze
Shone out in lovelight in the eye
Ere love had ever learn'd to sigh.

Hope strove to raise its song of cheer
As weary months made weary year ;
No Sunday bells, no house of prayer,
No priest of God gave blessing there.
What could they do each holy day
But strive, with dear ones far away,
To join in spirit in the Rite—
Earth's union with the Sons of Light?

Like daybreak from the tinted east
There came at last a zealous priest,
Restoring faith and hope's blest calm
In holy Church's soothing balm.
On altar rear'd in cabin shade
The Great Memorial was made,
And Bread of Life made hearts aglow
As in the old church long ago.

In Sacred Tide John's baby boy
Was made inheritor of joy.
It seem'd as if from home there came,
To cheer with light of heavenly flame,
The love of Mother Church, to bless
And cheer the gloomy wilderness.

The good priest, seeking scatter'd sheep,
Pass'd onward, and the shadows deep
Lay on the scenes of sorrow left,
Again of means of grace bereft.
Weeks pass away. The dark clouds spread,
The light is banish'd overhead,
And wild despair grows in the heart
That must from cherish'd treasure part.
The little child of love and grace,
And beautiful in limb and face,—
The ladder lifting earthly love
From earth up to its source above,—
Must be remov'd, that love alone
May centre round the Father's throne.

God took the little child to rest
Where manhood's trials no path infest,
With chrisom robe's unsullied glow
As spotless as the mountain's snow.
They clear'd a space in forest shade,
And there the little child was laid ;
No priest with benison was near,
No solemn service round the bier,—

Hearts break ! Why tarries blissful day,
When all the shadows flee away ?

An old man sat, and down his face
Hot tears each other seem'd to chase—
Not tears of sorrow, these no more
Could tax the burden of fourscore—
But tears of joy commingling fell,
And with the old man all was well.

Year after year arriv'd fresh bands
To clear the neighbouring forest lands ;
A town was rear'd, and stately fane,
That brought Old England back again,
With parish priest and chanting choir
And clanging music from the spire ;
And Mary's grave, that green was kept,
Close by where Mary's darling slept,
To-day, beneath the church bells' sound,
Becomes a part of holy ground.
To-day the mitr'd bishop bless'd
The new churchyard, where lov'd ones rest,
Then in the church in solemn state
Proceedëd all to consecrate,
Which done, burst forth in choral praise
The joy of Eucharistic lays.

The old man wept, for joy he wept,
In thought he once more boyhood kept.
At home he saw, as in a dream,
The white-rob'd throng, the altar's gleam,

The vested priest, the incense cloud,
And heard the *Gloria* pealing loud.
And truly in the church now rear'd
His boyhood linger'd, though betear'd,
The service never losing hold,
For Mother Church can ne'er grow old.
It was enough, his joy complete,
He could with one of old repeat
His *Nunc Dimittis*, till should cease
Earth's turmoil in the perfect peace.

Three graves, that eastward, homeward lie
Beneath the far Canadian sky,
Tell of the rest to pilgrim band
Who seek the new and better land.
God grant them light of endless day,
When sighs and sorrows flee away.

THE WIND.

THE wind came softly over the lea,
Bringing a message of love to me,
It bore on its breath the primrose scent,
And early flowers their fragrance lent ;
Its hidden lyre the whole day long
Gave warbling notes of the spring-birds' song
And the comfort of hope came floating by
To the music of winter's lullaby.

The zephyrs of summer came out to play,
And the insects buzzed in a roundelay,
While the lights on the ground where the forest
      grew
In merriest glee danc'd the whole day through,
And the gentle voice of summer was heard,
Where scarcely its breath the aspens stirr'd,
Assuring that life is not all that's drear
While summer's first course precedes autumn's
      cheer.

There came up a wind from the northern plain,
The faded leaves mark'd its pitiless train,
The flowers all died at its withering touch,
And the song-birds hid from its deadly clutch ;

But it brought the snow in a faltering shower
And the Christmas chimes from the old church
 tower,
And the dead earth's breast in its glittering white
To heaven reflected the snowy light.

And so, when the toil of the spring is o'er,
And summer in autumn fades more and more,
The bitter wind, coming with chilling breath
And leading the way to the gate of death,
Will surely the heavenly chimes awake,
That ever and ever sweet music make,
To usher the light of eternal glow
To the faithful soul in its robe of snow.

A LANDSCAPE.

RAVISHING beauty, stretch'd out to the sea !
Faultless mosaic of upland and lea !
Charm of the weary, the solace of age,
Painting Divine on the earth's sombre page !

Here, 'neath the shade of an o'erspreading tree,
Loveliness forms fairy garlands for me,
Gardens Queen Flora's bright glories enfold,
Buttercups weave me a carpet of gold.

Snows of the summer 'mong hawthorn leaves lie,
Bluebells are nodding as zephyrs creep by,
Far in expanse of the unchanging blue
Carols the lark in a song ever new.

Yonder the streamlet, a mirror of light,
Murmurs for ever its song of delight,
Dragon-flies poise o'er forget-me-not flowers,
O'er the dank grass are the dog-roses' bowers.

Cloth'd in a garb of the ivy's dark leaves,
Peeps the old manor-house forth from the trees,
Butterflies carelessly dance all the day
Where patchwork of blossoms makes brilliant dis-
    play.

Near stands a cottage where white roses cling,
Swallows around it are ever on wing,
While from its garden, with fragrance oppress'd,
Laughter of childhood makes music the best.

Far in the west, purpling into the skies,
Hills in succession eternally rise,
Surely from regions of nightfall to sever
Lands where the sunshine falls ever and ever.

Beautiful country of meadow and wood,
God in creation pronounces thee good !
Thou, His cathedral to echo along
Joyous and full Benedicite song.

THE BASS-VIOL.

THE church was musty, damp, and cold,
Its pews worm-eaten, dismal, old ;
White slabs on leaning walls record
The perfect lives of squire and lord.

On altar-tombs the shadows crept,
Where knights and dames in sculpture slept
'Neath rusty helm and banner torn,
That once in triumph had been borne.

And many a brass on pavement lay,
And urged the worshippers to pray
For souls of worthies, long gone hence
In holy faith and penitence.

The rector's voice in quavering sound
Recited holy prayers profound,
The clerk, as deputy, alone
Responded in a nasal tone.

In western gallery aloft
The village orchestra met oft
To practise, and from chime to chime
To argue points of tune and time.

On Sundays there, in triple row,
With frequent turns and measure slow—
While people turned in wondering gaze—
They led the choir in choral praise.

The strings and flutes in chords unite,
The singers sing with earnest might—
To them the well-worn Hundredth Psalm
Of all things is a constant charm.

One sturdy soul, well-nigh fourscore,
Had seen his jubilee and more
As bass-viol player, deep and clear,
And treat indeed to village ear.

How he enjoy'd, with steady bow,
To make the depths of music flow
In Christmas Hymn or Easter song,
Each final cadence making long !

The feeble rector, full of years,
Pass'd onward from this vale of tears,
To join the ranks of spirits blest
Who in God's Paradise find rest.

Succeeding rector changes made,
But none engender'd deeper shade
Than that which from the gallery sent
The strings and pipes to banishment.

The old bass-viol was pack'd away,
Its owner had no heart to play ;
Its occupation gone, he pined
In vain for aught to soothe his mind.

Like those of old by Babylon's stream,
His heart without a liv'ning gleam,
He could not in the Lord's song bear
For evermore his wonted share.

The old man wept—tears easy flow
From those far on life's road of woe—
But in his dreams he play'd again
The bass in each familiar strain.

His grandchild read the holy lore,
And from the Revelation's store
He drank in music of the throng,
Where golden harps assist the song.

He woke one morning cold and grey,
As eastern skies drove night away,
And told with joy-tears in his eye
How in the night a choir drew nigh.

Their golden harps and voices clear,
Accorded in a deathless sphere :
" Hark ! There again the music's made,
They want my dear bass-viol's aid ! "

So said he, and he pass'd away
Where, through the length of endless day,
Earth's discords end in heaven's new song,
And change can never work a wrong.

IN MEMORIAM.

REV. C. L. VAUGHAN, FOUNDER AND RECTOR OF CHRIST
CHURCH, ST. LEONARD'S-ON-SEA.

*As he was ascending the Julier Pass, on his way to a holiday
resort, God called him, August 8, 1895.*

Away in lands of mount and lake,
  Beyond the southern main,
He fain a resting time would take,
  Till duty called again.
But God in love gave sweeter rest,
Where all souls wait the vision blest.

Across the sea ! and safe at last,
  Beyond the billows' roar,
The waves of troubled life all past,
  He gains the peaceful shore,
Where shines the light that grows for aye,
Till dawns the Resurrection Day.

Amid the mighty mountains old,
  Snow-capped in summer ray,
God's angels glittering wings unfold,
  And swiftly bear away
The gentle soul to true life's rills,
That flow from everlasting hills.

No more for him earth's pilgrim hymns,
  But, nearer to the shrine,
Where angel-wafted incense dims
  The mystic lights Divine,
He hears the nine-fold orders raise
High heaven's Eucharistic lays.

There in a worship, one with ours,
  Still for his flock he prays,
That each may in the thornless bowers
  On fadeless glory gaze,
And priest and people e'er unite
In bliss of Beatific light.

AURORA BOREALIS.

Swift rustling from the courts of light
   Aurora's garments glow,
Awaking from the winter's night
   The sparkling gems of snow,

When lengthen'd shadows slowly fall
   Athwart the northern plain,
And spectre night its gloomy pall
   Spreads o'er the earth again,

When winter frowns through sullen skies,
   And icy fingers chill,
While virgin snow untrodden lies
   Upon the silent hill.

She dances on in mystic glee,
   Through halls of rainbow dye,
And, scatter'd on the ice-bound sea,
   Her fallen jewels lie.

She throws the gates of night aside,
   While glory passing by
Outspreads its ruddy pinions wide
   Across the glowing sky.

E'en so, when on the path of life
  The shadows darkly stray,
And hearts are broken in the strife
  As daylight dies away,—

When hearts in which our love would rest
  Are yielding no returns,
And winter snow falls on the breast
  That for the summer yearns,

And only night enwraps the grave
  Where hope long buried lies,
And stars withdraw the light they gave,
  As clouds enshroud the skies,—

There comes from fields of Paradise
  A strange unearthly glow,
The violets yield their odours sweet
  Beneath the chilly snow,

And happy memories, crowding round,
  Flood all the winter night,
The weary path o'er frozen ground
  To gladden with their light ;

Upon the earth-bound graves they lie
  As glow of Dawn of Day ;
They tell the promis'd morn is nigh,
  When shadows flee away.

SLEEP.

O soothing Sleep !
    That giv'st a calm retreat,
    When throbbing pulses beat,
    And tides of sorrow meet
            In strife !

Restoring hope
    To restless fever bed,
    Destroying woes that tread
    On joy's bright laughing head
            And life !

Strange Sleep ! to hush
    The din of daily strife,
    To calm the troubled life,
    And give, when fears are rife,
            Release !

To spread thy wing
    As comes the murky night,
    Where might attacks the right,
    And on contention light
            In peace !

On tossing ship,
  That braves the raging sea,
  A spell work'd out by thee
  Will make the storm to be
     A calm !

In prison cell,
  Though all be dark and drear,
  Though all be restless fear,
  All's well, if thou bring'st near
     Thy balm !

The travellers tir'd
  On many a dusty way,
  Faint in the sultry ray,
  In thy refreshing sway
     Find rest !

The outcast lone
  Seeks thine all-soothing hour,
  And woos thy magic power
  To weave a homeland bower
     The best.

The little child
  Will from its joyous play
  To thy enfolding stray,
  While angels watch alway
     Close by.

Yet when thy hand
>The robe of being rends,
>A shadow on thee tends,
>Thy subtle music lends
>>A sigh.

Say, is't that thou,
>With life-bereaving dart,
>The balm of sorrow's smart,
>The younger sister art
>>To Death ?

Yea, even so !
>Asleep our lov'd ones lie,
>But morning draweth nigh,
>When God gives, passing by
>>Life's breath !

ALLELUIA !

Borne on the incense-laden'd air
　With chords from harps of gold,
From temple throng in raiment fair
　The waves of music roll'd.

The burden of the sacred theme
　That woke the Psalmist's praise,
Anticipated as in dream
　The song of Christian days :—

Of days when life o'er death prevails
　And Calvary's gloom has fled,
When Easter Alleluia hails
　The Firstfruits of the dead.

And though perforce must pierce the skies
　Earth's Miserere's wail,
Yet Alleluias mingling rise
　As saints o'er sin prevail.

As when fierce hordes assail'd the land,
　And hearts in terror fail'd,
And stoutest in the Christian band
　Before the foemen quail'd,

When, with God's blessing hearts to cheer
  And noble deeds inspire,
The aged bishop's form drew near,
  Re-kindling dying fire,

The Christian hosts a welcome sang
  In Alleluias loud,
That in the wondering welkin rang
  And echo'd to the cloud,

And struck the chords of panic wide
  Th' invading hosts among,
Confusion, like the Red Sea tide,
  O'erwhelming dreaded throng ;—

E'en so the Christian soldier quells
  The foe in steadfast fight,
His Alleluia yet dispels
  The alien hosts of night.

From minster choir and village fane,
  Borne on the breath of song,
The angels gather up the strain
  Till swells the triumph song,

That, free from jarring sounds of night,
  Bears on its choral tide
The praise of all who stand in light
  That knows no eventide.

WHAT IS SORROW?

A WIDOW from the gate of Nain,
Chief mourner in the funeral train—
A mother, knowing all its pain,
                              Will tell.

In bitterness the sad ones weeping
For Lazarus in Death's arms now sleeping,
Where the tomb his dust is keeping,
                              Will tell.

The king,[1] whose fifteen years were run
Without a smile—in woe begun
And ended for his drownèd son—
                              Will tell.

The vanquish'd queen [2] amid her foes,
The wild despair her sad heart knows,
The burning anguish of her woes
                              Will tell.

The livid face and furtive glance,
Befitting not the child of France,[3]
The tears that down his pale cheeks dance
                              Will tell.

[1] Henry I.   [2] Margarét of Anjou.   [3] The Dauphin.

What is it ?   Who the wide world o'er
But must support its burden sore,
Yet who possesses needful lore
                    To say ?

'Tis like a shadow where we tread,
A spectre in the maze we thread,
That hovers close till with the dead
                    We sleep.

EVENTIDE.

THE sunlight dies from out the western sky,
And sombre twilight slowly passes by,
Sweet lingering on the happy silence dwells
The dying cadence of the village bells,
And from the grove, borne ever and anon,
The blackbird's evensong still ringeth on.
Each watchful star hangs out its taper light,
The wind reposes on the breast of night,
By dewdrops sooth'd the daisy falls asleep,
The nightingales in hawthorn vigils keep.
The day is spent.   Come, Lord, at eventide,
And in the silent hours with us abide.

THE EVERLASTING HILLS.

FAR off, and hid by clouds that hover near
To veil the peaks, like garment of the seer,
The mountains bow in awe each craggy head
And tremble as the lightning flash is shed.

Cloth'd in the mist,—for secrets deep amid
Their ever-brooding solitude are hid—
Like hermits lifted from earth's changing state
They in God's presence ever stand and wait.

They heard the last communing with his God
When desert road to Canaan's land was trod,
And knew the spot where God that servant laid
When angel hands the sepulchre had made.

They know Whose Hand unlock'd that unknown
    grave
And back to earth the meekest hero gave
To join Elias, as the cloud o'erspread,
In worshipping the Lord of quick and dead.

Far off but yesterday, and now so nigh,
They almost echo back our sorrow's cry
To rest for ever, lifted from earth's care,
And in the silence heavenly visions share.

Full oft the misty cowl is cast aside,
In noontide glory endless snows abide,
And when below the twilight shadows creep
The glowing light still crowns the rugged steep.

So God's dear saints, when closes chequer'd day,
Uplifted as the evening shadows stray,
Are bath'd in splendour of the fadeless light
That ever banishes the shroud of night.

From out the mountain glacier's icy hand
Escape the streams that feed the thirsty land,
And I, in impotence, lift longing eyes
To those fair hills whence spring the soul's supplies.

And as encompass'd stands the city blest,
Hills keeping guard, that none may dare molest,
So God around His people evermore
Protection gives when swells the battle's roar.

THE LITTLE GRAVE.

"Here I and Sorrow sit."—*King John.*

'Twas nothing but a little mound
  Of hallow'd ground,
'Twas but a very tiny grave
  Where willows wave,
And costly marble had it not :—
  Few mark'd the spot—
" 'Tis but a child's grave," so they said,
  And onward sped.

And yet 'twas wet with many tears,
  For hope of years,
The child of many a fervent prayer
  Was buried there.
Few marked the spot, yet one oft made
  The willow shade
A resting-place, and vigils kept
  Where " Baby " slept.

That mother calls it not a mound
  Of churchyard ground,
Nor calls that spot where willows wave
  " A little grave,"

'Tis more,—'tis to her heart more dear
        Than all earth's gear—
For 'neath that casket's grassy lid
        Love's treasure's hid. .

And so on sorrow's throne she waits ;
        The grave's closed gates
Will ope when sorrow's reign is past,
        And give at last
Reunion, where the pure in heart
        No more may part,
And broken hearts find healing blest
        In heaven's dear rest.

IN MEMORIAM, A. M.

Obit., February 17, 1895, *aged* 80.

THE glittering snow had cloth'd the hills,
   Ice-bound the waters lay,
And bitter winds through leafless woods
   Moan'd all the winter day,
But from the snow and chilling blast
Our dear one to God's haven pass'd.

The dull earth sigh'd to skies of grey,
   We yearn'd for days of spring,
For sunshine's glory and the joys
   Earth's first-born flow'rets bring,
But she sought rest where angels sing
The song of everlasting spring.

The fleeting years of life had run
   In chequer'd light and shade,
O'er rugged heights and thorn-set plains
   The pilgrim pathway stray'd,
But in the land of spirits blest
The weary ones find welcome rest.

Earth's near and dearest one by one
  Departed from her side,
And heart of love was oft o'erwhelm'd
  In rush of sorrow's tide,
But in the light of yonder shore
She gains her near and dear once more.

And so, commending her to God,
  That He in endless light
May give the fulness of all joy
  In Beatific sight,
We wait the end of sorrow's reign
And then receive her back again.

THE SEAMLESS ROBE.

A SEAMLESS robe He wore, Whose life divine
One purpose wove in charity benign,
To knit earth's scatter'd children lovingly
In Holy Church, a seamless robe to be.

The seamless robe! Will Schism's daring hand
Attempt to rend it, tearing strand from strand?
Lord, pity those who set at naught Thy plea
That in Thy Church all may be one in Thee.

The seamless robe! A touch upon its hem
Brought back to fainting heart health's lustrous
    gem,
Restoring peace and happiness again
Where hopeless life was wearing out in pain.

So in the garment of Thy presence here,
In Sacramental robe for us draw near,
That sin-sick souls may touch, and find release
As virtue from Thee yields Thy perfect peace.

Dear Christ, Whose raiment on far Tabor's height
Outshone the splendour of the noontide light,
So clothe us here with garments of Thy grace,
That we at last may see Thee face to face.

"AND THERE WAS NO MORE SEA."

Thou mighty ever-changing sea,—
  Now calm as child asleep,
Anon in rage a war to wage
  With winds that o'er thee sweep ;

Now bearing tints of heaven-born blue,
  Anon the cloudy shade
In ebb and flow no rest to know
  Since first divinely made,—

Thou hast a fitting place, where nought
  Continues in one stay,
And grief and joy in strange alloy
  Commingle day by day.

But comes a world before whose joys
  The ills of this world flee,
Where none may know the cloud of woe
  And there shall be no sea.

Old ocean, stretching endlessly,
  Divides the near and dear,
And on its shore eyes evermore
  Are dim with many a tear.

But there's a land of endless love
  Where partings cannot be,—
The farewell word shall ne'er be heard
  When there is no more sea.

The angry waves in fury dash
  Around the sinking bark,
The anguish cries in storm-winds rise
  Above the waters dark.

Deep ocean, in thy cold embrace
  Is many a secret grave,
Where corals grow in ruddy glow
  Beneath thy restless wave.

The mother breaks her heart at home
  For one the wreck had borne ;
For pining grief no kind relief
  Bids lovers cease to mourn.

But in the fatherland of life
  There'll be no place for thee,—
No mourner's cry—no death to die—
  " There shall be no more sea."

A LAMENT.

My heart is sad and broken,
    The day is cold,
The clouds their tears are shedding
    On autumn's gold.
My little child lies dead, and all my weeping
Restores him not again to my fond keeping.

No more I hear the prattle's
    Enchanting sound,
That scattered far the worries
    E'er hovering round ;
No more for me the light all joy enhancing
That radiated from his full eyes' glancing.

My flow of tears is blinding,
    My hope has died !
List ! Is a whispering angel
    By my side,
With breathings blest to me the message telling
The Lord hath need of him in His bright dwelling?

" Dost thou not find life's journey
    Beset with woe,
Thy sword for ever battling
    With many a foe ?
Then love forbids thy grief at that swift winging,
Where nothing mars the harmony upspringing.

"Grudge not the King of Glory
　　　True purity ;
Grudge not the little children
　　　Felicity ;
But rather praise that He His dear love showeth
In choosing such to follow where He goeth.

"Thy child's dear love as ever
　　　Round thee twines,
Intensified and growing,
　　　It ever shines ;
It speaks, in tender accents ever calling,
To cheer thy steps and stay thy feet from falling.

"And evermore uprising,
　　　As incense sweet,
His prayers for thee surrounding
　　　The Mercy Seat
Prevail that thou, from strength to strength pro-
　　gressing,
Mayest share with him the Beatific blessing.

"When in the bliss of dying
　　　The curtain rends,
Thy little child awaiting
　　　Dear welcome tends,
That makes amends for all the pilgrim sadness,
And ushers in a day of cloudless gladness."

CHRISTMAS.

Bring the holly's blushing store,
Trailing ivy frosted o'er,
Laurustinus' leaves and flowers
Pluck'd from forest-shelter'd bowers,
Deck the church, the cot, the hall,
Weaving Christmas joy for all.

Ring, ye bells, ring loud and long,
Wafting on the angels' song ;
Winter winds repeat the strain,
Peace to earth comes back again,
Truth and mercy now unite,
Turning darkness into light.

Gather where the joy-bells ring
Birthday welcome to the King,
Kneel before Emmanuel's Shrine—
Bethlehem, with Food Divine—
There in grateful homage pray,
" Be Thou born in me to-day."

Call around the yule-log's blaze,
Gather'd as in bygone days,
All the homesteads near and dear,
One in heart, as one in cheer,
Banish ev'ry thought of care
By the love-light gleaming there.

Let sweet charity have sway,
Strife be still'd, feuds done away ;
Feed the hungry, make the sad
With thy Christmas sunshine glad ;
For the crumbs the children fling
Birds will cheer the coming spring.

A CHRISTMAS WISH.

"ON EARTH PEACE."

MAY Christmas chimes, that through the air
    Ring in the Natal Feast,
Before the streams of morning flow
    Across the sleeping east,
To thee bear on their magic wing
The peace the Christmas tidings bring!

When in the calm of morning hour,
    Incarnate Love draws near,
May His blest Presence quicken love,
    Thy falt'ring footsteps cheer,
And bid the Anthem never cease
That soothes with everlasting peace.

When loud the chancel's vested choir
    Takes up the Christmas strain,
And in the joy of Christmastide
    Sings Bethlehem's song again
Of praise to God in highest heaven,
And peace to sin-stain'd mortals given,

May music, rising in the soul,
    A spell of gladness send,
A foretaste of that Eucharist
    That never has an end,
Where, in eternal festal light,
Are banished minor songs of night!

When round the old home's ruddy glow
    Meet near and dear again,
And hearts long severed forge once more
    New links in true love's chain,
May all be foretastes of the love
Unbroken in the home above !

And when the swelling last Amen
    Is closing evensong,
And decorated arch and aisle
    Its dying notes prolong,
Full richly may God's peace descend
And in thy life its blessings blend.

EASTER.

'Tis Easter Day, and earth awakes
   In Resurrection lays ;
The Church below her garment takes
   Of beauty and of praise,
From Patmos fixing longing eye
On her Jerusalem on high.

Where glad procession sweeps along
   The streets of shining gold,
And waves of an ecstatic song,
   By ceaseless echoes roll'd,
All break upon th' eternal shore
In Alleluias evermore.

The hosts redeem'd, in fair array,
   With palms of triumph wend,
And in the light of endless day
   The Lamb Divine attend,
Who, once the Leader in the strife,
Now leads beside the stream of life.

And where, before the Altar Throne,
   The full-voiced choir has place,
Where Mercy's rainbow light is thrown
   And God reveals His Face,
Where harps a faultless strain outpour
And prostrate worshippers adore.

In antiphon the Seraphs sing,
  "Thrice Holy, Lord most high,"
The angels bend 'neath glittering wing
  And swell the vocal cry,
And all the saints uniting raise
The song of everlasting praise.

Seven wond'rous Lights cast gladdening beams,
  Though night can never be,
Their radiant glory ever streams
  Upon the crystal sea,
O'er which from angels' wafting hand
The fragrant incense clouds expand.

O blissful vision of the rest
  In store when wand'rings cease !
O happy portion of the blest
  In thy dear home of peace !
God grant when this life's Lent is o'er
Thine Eastertide for evermore !

ASCENSION DAY.

TRUE Manhood now ascendeth,
  Our Jacob and our Head,
To gather earth's tired members—
  His feet[1]—into the bed
Of never-fading glory
  Prepar'd for all the blest,
Who after days of toiling
  Rejoice in endless rest.

Our Joseph claims his Goshen,
  That, in its lambent light,
We, own'd by Him as brethren,
  May in His joys unite.
Our Solomon in glory,
  Now crown'd with regal gold,
To pilgrim band from Sheba
  Reveals delights untold.

As Priest toward the altar
  His Sacrifice to plead,
Our Christ in glory passes
  For us to intercede,
The choir of holy angels
  The festal introit sings,
While rolling cloud of incense
  From angel-censer springs.

[1] Genesis xlix. 33.

As Conqueror returning—
  Great Victor in the fight—
All alien hosts repelling
  And foes all put to flight—
He claims the crown of triumph,
  The Name all names above,
And from earth's ransom'd people
  Their grateful hearts of love.

" Unfold, eternal portals,
  For Glory's King make way,
Receive the Lord of battles
  To reign in endless day !"
"Who is the King of Glory ?"
  " 'Tis He the Church's Head,
The King in battle mighty,
  Who liveth and was dead."

For Him the warder angels
  The massive gates unfold,
And through the eternal city's
  Fair streets of burnish'd gold
The great procession passes,
  As all the joy-bells ring
To welcome Man to glory
  In Jesus, Lord and King.

CHILDREN'S FESTAL HYMN.

As of old palm-bearing throng
Raised the loud Hosannah song,
As of old the Temple's praise
Echo'd from the children's lays,
So to-day our lips proclaim
Glory to the Holy Name.
Honour, praise, for ever be
Jesus, Saviour, unto Thee.

Thou on earth a little Child,
Subject to Thy Mother mild,
Hast become the children's Friend
Ever loving to the end ;
Therefore we, who bear Thy Sign,
Yield ourselves as wholly Thine,
And in praising Thee unite
With the choirs of heavenly light.

Ever growing in Thy grace,
Striving in the heavenly race,
May our lives be hymns of joy,
Full of love without alloy !
Thus, beneath Thy guiding hand
Onward to the promised land,
We shall serve Thee and adore
Praising Thee for evermore.

Soon the pilgrim song will cease,
Warrior hosts shall rest in peace,
When earth's praises fade away
In the songs of endless day.
Lord, to Thee we glory give,
Ever with Thee may we live,
Praising with Thine angel host
Father, Son, and Holy Ghost. Amen.

"GRANT US THY PEACE."

HOLY JESUS, Lamb of God,
Blessed Saviour, loving Lord,
Hear us, trusting in Thy Word,
      And grant us peace.

In the busy hum of life,
When the Tempter's wiles are rife,
Soothe the weary in the strife
      With blessed peace.

As the tempest hovers near
And our spirits shrink with fear,
Then Thy trembling servants hear,
      And grant Thy peace.

When the broken spirit cries,
When the conscience bleeding lies,
And the tears of anguish rise,
      Oh ! grant Thy peace.

When the earth is cold and drear,
Lost the friends the heart held dear,
Come, dear Lord, the darkness cheer
      With Thy blest peace.

When declines our evening sun,
As the day of life is done,
And the journey almost run,
      Still grant Thy peace.

When the shadows round us stray,
Prince of Peace, be Thou our stay
Till we find in endless day
      Thy perfect peace.

HYMN.

*Sung at the Laying of the Foundation Stone of S. Mark's
Mission Hall, September 17, 1887.*

O CHRIST, our One Foundation,
  Thy blessing on us send,
That this, the work Thou givest,
  In good success may end.

Grant that each trusting servant
  Who here hath lent to Thee,
With Thine own loving portion
  Repaid again may be.

Have all within Thy keeping
  Who work this house to raise,
That they preserv'd in safety
  May yield Thee lives of praise.

May all now here assembled,
  In bonds of charity,
As living stones and holy
  Be built, O Lord, in Thee.

Here by Thy Spirit's power
  Thy lov'd lost sheep restore,
And bring them from their wanderings
  To leave Thy fold no more.

Here may Thy lambs be tended
  And brought up in Thy fear,
Be Thou in love the Teacher
  And draw the children near.

May love's cords here be strengthen'd
  In happy brotherhood,
And drooping hearts made joyful
  In fellowship of good.

We praise Thee and we bless Thee
  In whom redemption came,
With Father and the Spirit,
  To endless years the same.   Amen.

HYMN.

Sung at the Dedication of S. Mark's Mission Hall,
April 14, 1888.

LORD of Glory, King of Love,
We, with all Thy hosts above,
Lift our hearts, loud anthems raise
Thy Thrice-holy Name to praise.
Untold mercies crowd our way,
Grace is shower'd day by day,
For success that Thou hast given,
Grateful hearts we lift to Heaven.

Let Thy blessing ever be
On this house now built for Thee ;
May it to Thy glory tend,
And Thy Kingdom here extend ;
Here may souls be gather'd in,
Rescued from a life of sin,
Growing day by day in grace,
Till they reach Thy dwelling-place.

Bless the preaching of Thy Word,
Let the lisping prayer be heard,
Thy blest promises fulfil,
As we wait upon Thy will.

Let the children, as they learn,
Feel their hearts within them burn,
Gathering manna day by day,
Jesus with them on the way.

Let Thy people willingly
Here glad offerings make to Thee,
Holding fast Thy gracious word,
Lending substance to the Lord :
Thou hast taught that they who feed
Hungry brethren in their need
Do their deeds of love to Thee—
Thou their great reward shalt be.

When Thy temple rais'd on high
Gains its topstone gloriously,
Then may we by Thy dear grace
In that building have a place.
Fashion'd by its Architect
May we, with Thine own elect,
Praise for aye with angel host
Father, Son, and Holy Ghost.   Amen.

LITANY FOR S. ALBAN'S DAY.

HOLY LORD of mighty host,
Ever guarding Israel's coast,
Father, Son, and Holy Ghost;
> Hear us, Holy Trinity.

Jesu, in Whose Light now stand
Victor saints, a noble band,
Resting in the peaceful land;
> Hear us, Holy Jesu.

Thou, Whose strength gave Alban might
To the death to wage the fight,—
England's first on blood-stain'd height;
> Hear us, Holy Jesu.

Grant that, holding Thee in sight,
Wearing all God's armour bright,
We may conquer hosts of night;
> We beseech Thee, Jesu.

Be our Strength in Food Divine,
Thy mysterious Bread and Wine,
That we may be wholly Thine;
> We beseech Thee, Jesu.

'Neath Thy banner, brave and strong,
Through the battle, fierce and long,
Lead us on to victors' song ;
　　　　　We beseech Thee, Jesu.

When we lay our armour down,
Grant to each the fadeless crown,
With Thy Soldier of renown ;
　　　　　We beseech Thee, Jesu.

LITANY FOR A BOYS' GUILD.

God the Father, throned on high,
Lo ! Thy children now draw nigh ;
Listen to our humble cry ;
> Hear us, Holy Father.

God the Son, to Thee we plead,
Ever for us intercede—
In our danger and our need ;
> Save us, Holy Jesu.

God the Holy Ghost, to Thee,
We in solemn Litany
Pray for Thy blest purity ;
> Guide us, Holy Spirit.

Father, Son, and Spirit, blest
By Thy Church one God confess'd,
Lead us to Thy people's rest ;
> Spare us, Holy Trinity.

Jesu, once like us, a boy—
Like, yet free from sin's alloy,
Blessèd Mary's sweetest joy ;
> Hear us, Holy Jesu.

Chiefest Shepherd, dearest Friend,
Who hast promis'd to defend
And sustain us to the end ;
                     Hear us, Holy Jesu.

Who didst in the world prepare
Pastures for us, fresh and fair,
For Thy priests to feed us there ;
                     Hear us, Holy Jesu.

Who in love dost e'er abide
By the font's pure cleansing tide—
Precious water from Thy side ;
                     Hear us, Holy Jesu.

Who didst there join us to Thee
In Thy Church's unity,
That we might Thy members be ;
                     Hear us, Holy Jesu.

Who to nourish life there given
Hast Thy precious body riven,
Giving us the Bread of Heaven ;
                     Hear us, Holy Jesu.

Perfect Victim, true High Priest,
Who from sin hath man released
Heavenly Bread, on Whom we feast ;
                     Hear us, Holy Jesu.

Tree of Life, true living Vine,
Veil'd in form of Bread and Wine,—
Nourishment and Strength divine ;
.   Hear us, Holy Jesu.

Bless our union, may it prove
Constant bond of Christian love,
Foretaste of Thy courts above ;
                     We beseech Thee, Jesu.

Keep us in the narrow way ;
Watch and guard us, lest we stray ;
Keep us children of the day ;
                     We beseech Thee, Jesu.

May no spot of sin appear
On our white baptismal gear,
May no evil hover near ;
                     We beseech Thee, Jesu.

When afflicted for Thy sake
May we straightway all forsake,
Glad with Thee Thy cross to take ;
                     We beseech Thee, Jesu.

Haste our Confirmation hour,
When Thy Spirit comes with power,
Comfort, strength, and richest dower ;
                     We beseech Thee, Jesu.

When Thou see'st 'tis fit and good,
Feed us with Thine Altar-food—
Precious Body, precious Blood ;
> We beseech Thee, Jesu.

May our souls then strengthen'd be,
And our life renew'd in Thee,
Never more decay to see ;
> We beseech Thee, Jesu.

When we meet temptation sore,
When, with grief, Thine aid implore,
And in tears our sin deplore ;
> Save us, Holy Jesu.

In the hour when we must die,
In our last dread agony,
Lord, do Thou Thy grace supply ;
> Save us, Holy Jesu.

May all those who still remain
Outcasts in the world's domain,
At Thy font be born again ;
> Save *them*, Holy Jesu.

And in love do Thou restore
Wanderers from Thy Church's lore,—
Let them never wander more ;
> Save *them*, Holy Jesu.

When the Heavens shall roll away
On the dreadful judgment day,
Lord of Mercy, be our stay ;

        Save us, Holy Jesu.

UNWIN BROTHERS, PRINTERS, WOKING AND LONDON.